I0463856

Last Year's Words, and Next Year's Voices

ESSAYS AND SPEECHES FROM
A DECADE AS CHAIRMAN
OF THE INTERNATIONAL
CONFERENCE OF SYMPHONY
AND OPERA MUSICIANS

BRUCE RIDGE

Copyright © 2018 Bruce Ridge.

All rights reserved. No part of this book may be reproduced, stored, or
transmitted by any means—whether auditory, graphic, mechanical,
or electronic—without written permission of the author, except in the
case of brief excerpts used in critical articles and reviews. Unauthorized
reproduction of any part of this work is illegal and is punishable by law.

This book is a work of non-fiction. Unless otherwise noted, the author and the publisher
make no explicit guarantees as to the accuracy of the information contained in this book
and in some cases, names of people and places have been altered to protect their privacy.

ISBN: 978-1-4834-8836-3 (sc)
ISBN: 978-1-4834-8835-6 (e)

Library of Congress Control Number: 2018908208

Because of the dynamic nature of the Internet, any web addresses or links contained in
this book may have changed since publication and may no longer be valid. The views
expressed in this work are solely those of the author and do not necessarily reflect the
views of the publisher, and the publisher hereby disclaims any responsibility for them.

Lulu Publishing Services rev. date: 7/20/2018

Contents

Essays

Selected speeches

Foreword

BY MEREDITH SNOW

ICSOM CHAIRPERSON (2016-)

The ten years that Bruce Ridge served as Chairman of ICSOM, from 2006 to 2016, were probably the most economically challenging that our orchestras had faced since ICSOM was formed in 1962. The dot-com recession of 2001 and the 'Great Recession' in 2008 left behind a wake of devastation in the American economy. Our orchestras were hit particularly hard. Endowments were laid waste by the stock market crash, economic instability shook the confidence of donors, and ill-advised real estate ventures became a financial albatross for several orchestras. The already existing presentiment of the "unsustainability" and "irrelevance" of classical orchestras became a deluge of negative messaging, not just from the press, but from the very managers and boards charged with preserving these institutions.

Bruce was a beacon of light in these troubled times. Not only was his leadership an inspiration to our musicians, reminding us of the invaluable contribution we make to our communities, but he also mitigated the defeatist dialogue surrounding our industry. By unceasingly drawing attention to the economic and educational benefits of sustaining an orchestra—with facts not rhetoric— he turned the tide of pessimism that threatened to marginalize our profession.

Wherever an orchestra was in trouble, Bruce was there to advise and support the musicians, often speaking with management and the board as well. He began the "Call to Action" donations to support orchestras during work stoppages. Over the course of his ten-year chairmanship, he spoke at numerous conferences, schools, and conservatories, and spread his positive message to thousands of people. Herein are many of his published essays and speeches, as relevant today as when they were written.

Bruce has been a great leader for ICSOM and for our industry. He is a tireless advocate of the arts, of orchestras and of the need to support music education. His dedication to our ICSOM orchestras is unparalleled. It has been a privilege to have served with him on the Governing Board for so many years, and I am honored to call him my friend.

Introduction

BRUCE RIDGE
JUNE 2018

Very early in his career, Bob Dylan wrote "Do not create anything. It will be misinterpreted. It will not change. It will follow you the rest of your life."

In the nearly two years since I stepped down as ICSOM Chair, the question people ask most often is, "What are you doing now?" Primarily, I have been reading. It has been a great luxury. If it is true that we like to buy books because we think we are buying the time to read them, it has been a great gift that, after so many years of activism, I have actually had such time.

About a year into this phase of relative retirement, I began reading the essays and speeches I wrote from my time with ICSOM, some of which are now over a decade old, and some of which seemed new to my memory. Yes, they have not changed, and yes, some were misinterpreted at the time, but each one took on a new role for me as I revisited the writing, and the time in which the pieces were written. Some were like snapshots; Polaroids of memories that reminded me more of the people I met in a decade of travel than the difficulties we were facing as classical musicians. I was fortunate to work with incredible artists who demonstrated bravery and resiliency at a time when the economy melded with years of negative rhetoric to endanger these musical institutions to which we have dedicated our lives.

But these memories did not seem to live entirely in the past for me. These pages report on difficulties and triumphs, and serve as cautionary tales in a field that tends to emphasize the study of failure above the replication of success. Many of the orchestras that faced the greatest crises have emerged stronger, eager to embrace the tremendous successes they have achieved in the ensuing years.

In working on these issues that faced our field, we wanted to elevate the tone of the debate. We wanted to emphasize hope, and beauty, and we wanted to unite together to believe it was possible to realize our dreams, and perhaps more importantly, to recognize that no hardship could diminish those dreams for true artists.

Even in a mere two years, the world has changed. While orchestral musicians emerged from the recession more unified and more supportive of each other in times of need, it is difficult to avoid being affected by the destructive level of discourse that has descended upon the world in all areas of political and social life.

In this moment of civilization, where the incessant drone of news seems to embrace a rhetoric of hatred, dishonesty, and distrust among the citizens of the world, our music remains more relevant than ever.

Despite the challenges that now face the world, what emerges for me in reflecting upon these essays is the successes that were achieved by the musicians who unified to save their orchestras, and enrich their presence in their cities. Entirely new forms of media emerged over the decade, and musicians learned to utilize these new tools for a new era of positive advocacy. And while many destructive tactics were used against musicians in a time of economic difficulties for orchestras (perhaps most notably an unprecedented spate of lockouts) we did not merely survive; we grew.

It should be said that there is some repetition in these pages, which is inevitable as we sought to emphasize so many themes to stay on message. The speeches I delivered especially tended to harvest from essays I was writing at the time. But there are many memories for me here as well.

I remember pacing the campus of the University of Michigan in 2012, the night before delivering the keynote address at the American Orchestra Summit, in what would serve as both my most controversial and perhaps my proudest moment as ICSOM Chair. I remember a similar evening walking the streets of Washington, DC in 2009, the night before my testimony before Congress. But it is the visits with musicians that I remember most vividly and there were moments of hope offered by the strength of our membership that will sustain me always.

There remain many causes before us that require our participation, both for our orchestras and our place in the world. In my final essay as ICSOM Chair I quoted from an opinion piece in *The Etude* from 1947: "The time has long since passed when musicians were expected to stand submissively, as 'souls apart' outside the gates of world progress, and not participate in the tremendous movements of the age...the participation of musically trained minds cannot fail to be of priceless value to the body politic at this startling moment in world history."

We will never be fearful; we will never be isolated; we will never be apathetic. A decade of travel and a decade of evenings spent with the artists of the world convinced me that musicians accomplish amazing and beautiful things on a nightly basis. With every day that passes I am even more convinced that the world needs to hear our music and our voices as never before.

Prelude:

LAST YEAR'S WORDS, AND NEXT YEAR'S VOICES

Last Year's Words, and Next Year's Voices

SENZA SORDINO
DECEMBER, 2013

In February of 1979, I joined my first professional orchestra at the age of fifteen. I remember everything about the night of my first concert, and I still have the program as if to prove it really happened. I remember how my 100% polyester tuxedo didn't fit all that well, and how my giant bow tie was probably more appropriate for those awkward senior prom photographs than for the orchestra's attire. I remember the feel of backstage, and the names of everyone on stage with me that night. I was joining a great orchestra, one that was composed of my teachers and mentors. I idolized them, and now they were graciously indulging and tolerating me by allowing me to join them. Walking on stage was so exciting that I kept going back off stage, just so I could experience walking on stage again.

I remember that after the concert, there was a temporary bar in the lobby, selling small glasses of wine. I ordered a glass, and of course they questioned my age. But I replied with a huff and an indignation that only a 15-year-old can muster, saying "I'm in the orchestra." So, with some pretty apparent reluctance, they went ahead and served me. (I am assuming the statute of limitations has expired.)

I stood there that night thinking that absolutely anything was possible, and decades later I remain haunted by that potential.

Do you know what I mean by "the mirage in the road"? It's that shimmering illusion of water that taunts you on the highway about 25 yards in front of your car on hot humid days. On the coast of North Carolina, the salt air and humidity combine to make the mirage appear especially intense and enticing. I used to get frustrated with my father for not driving fast enough to catch up to the shimmering pool of water. I swore that, when I was older, I would catch the mirage. I could even imagine the splash as I caught up to it, drove through it, and left it behind.

With the arrival of the new year, literally on January 1, I will be fifty years old. I feel as if a threshold has been crossed, and I'm not certain of what lies ahead of me, or for that matter, what lingers behind.

On that first night back in 1979, there was meaning in everything I saw, heard, and touched. Every note of music seemed to mean more than the last. I sensed that a new age of enlightenment was about to ease the world's burdens. Music, art, poetry, compassion, love, empathy—these seemed to be the most important things. I was surrounding myself with people who all felt the same way and who were eager to live in ways that would allow them to approach expressing the inexpressible.

One of the Flying Wallendas once said: "Life is on the wire. The rest is just waiting."

I want it back. I want to feel again the excitement I felt when I was hearing music for the first time; I want to be a part of an idealistic community that only musicians can truly create as we live and work together, and I want to believe again, with apologies to Keats, that the truth and beauty to which we aspire is still within reach.

As musicians we invest our lives in the pursuit of beauty, spending our days (and especially our nights) reaching for something we all know is greater than ourselves. It is all the more remarkable that we still believe at all, despite working in a field that is so ugly at times.

In a field that offers the world beauty, peace, solace, inspiration, and communion, the sounds of our instruments and the voices of Mozart, Beethoven, and Brahms must work to be heard over a din of destructive negativity, where self-promoting and self-fulfilling advocates of the demise of music engage in meaningless personal attacks, and a handful of divisive and polarizing figures attempt to dictate the future based on the tenets of their failed pasts. But one thing I have learned in life is that what you allow to continue is what will continue, so we must never allow the negative voices to silence us, either as musicians or as citizens of the world.

I have also learned another truth: people always overplay their hands.

Those who deal a negative hand will not be heard, will not be remembered, and through the passing of time will be proven to have been on the wrong side of history.

That is not to say though that change is not required; change must be welcomed in all endeavors. And while I am indulgently reflective for the moment, I think we sometimes approach the future while still facing the past. All of our organizations must change, and every facet of our lives must be ready and eager to adapt. Constant change is here to stay, and I've recently heard it said that "only a fool trips on what is behind him."

Answers may be found in the past, but solutions are found in the future.

Life can be a process of learning how to live with disappointment while still allowing yourself to hope. I find my hope in the next generation of musicians, many not yet born when I repeatedly walked on and off stage that first night in 1979. I see and hear in these musicians the same belief that I had then, and there is no part of me that wants to teach them to doubt. I am not at all eager to tell them "how things really are."

Actually, I'm kind of hoping that they will remind me of how things could be. Some of the leaders and musicians I am working with had not even touched a musical instrument when I joined my current orchestra. Yet I do not doubt that they will achieve far greater things, through music and through ICSOM, than I could have dreamt even all those years ago.

In every orchestra I have joined, I was the youngest member for a while. In 2006 I was the youngest person to become ICSOM chair. Such accolades are past me now. As George Carlin said "You can't tell time; time tells you." Still, I want to chase the mirage in the road again, and imagine my wheels splashing through the water as I leave all illusions behind—even if my fifty years have tried to convince me that the goals I once set for myself will always remain ahead of me.

"For last year's words belong to last year's language, and
next year's words await another voice." – T.S. Eliot

I wish you all a brave New Year.
With love and admiration,
Bruce

Essays

2006-2016

Lessons from Nashville

SENZA SORDINO
OCTOBER, 2006

In the few moments during the 2006 ICSOM Conference that did not find me in meetings, I was able to sneak away from the hotel and venture into the streets of Nashville. This was my first visit to this city, and I was eager to hear as much music as I could in the clubs that line Nashville's Broadway. I had learned and played a lot of this music when I was growing up, especially in Southside Virginia. I knew that Bob Dylan had come here to record three classic albums and to work with Johnny Cash. I knew that I was walking past bars where Willie Nelson had bought drinks for Patsy Cline. These streets veritably drip with music, with a band in every bar. Those who weren't booked were playing on the street. There were well-groomed boys in suits and toothless blues guitar players who seemed as though they could have been sent by central casting. And all of these people could play! It was exhilarating to see and hear a city so alive with music.

Making my way back to the downtown Hilton where the conference was being held, I was stunned for a moment when I looked through an alleyway to see the Schermerhorn Symphony Center—a gleaming building against the night sky, just weeks from opening. The delegates to the Conference had already received a tour, and many of us were convinced that it is one of the most impressive halls we have ever visited. Beautifully appointed in every way, it has delicate features and just about every amenity imaginable to enhance the performance environment for the musicians.

As I stood there looking through that alley at the grand building, at first it seemed to clash with the music from the bars of Broadway. But then, I realized that the "City of Music" was only further investing in its heritage. These blocks of downtown Nashville have been revitalized with music. Reveling in the history of the Ryman Auditorium (the original Grand Ole Opry) and the street of dreams for songwriters of all styles, it makes perfect sense that Music City USA would build such a beautiful monument to its symphony orchestra. This downtown revitalization is fantastic. The arena where the Nashville Predators play is right next to the Country Music Hall of Fame, which is across from the beautiful downtown Hilton, and now the block is completed by the $120 million home for the Nashville Symphony.

We must remember the history of this organization. Just 18 years ago the Nashville Symphony was in bankruptcy, facing dissolution. Then the citizens of Nashville came to the assistance of this city's own orchestra. There are too many heroes in this story to mention them all. But among them were the symphony's great benefactor, Martha Ingram, Local 257's legendary President Harold Bradley (the newest member of the Country Music Hall of Fame) and other country legends, and, most importantly, the musicians of the Nashville Symphony themselves. These musicians believed in their orchestra and their community. They worked to bring together a management that could share in the dreams of Nashville, and they have all delivered.

It is perfectly clear, however, that they have not built a museum. They have erected a building in which symphonic music will live, flourish, and be celebrated—just as so many other styles of music are celebrated a block or two away. Imagine what this will mean for their city. The area of downtown that the city leaders had so desired to revitalize is now thriving with restaurants and hotels, all of which will benefit from those attending concerts at the Schermerhorn Symphony Center. The businesses that surround the Center will profit as a result of the popularity of the orchestra, and the city will benefit from tax revenues of those spending their time, and money, downtown.

Those patrons will not just be spending money; they will be making an investment with the expectations of dividends. And they will be richly rewarded. They will prosper as their city prospers, their spirits will be uplifted by the great music so beautifully performed by the Nashville

Symphony, and they will take pride that the name of their great community has been spread worldwide through countless articles about how this great city of music has made such a bold statement. Their statement is clear, that symphonic music can and must succeed alongside every kind of music, every kind of business, and every kind of cultural hyacinth for the soul.

All of this grew from the dark time of bankruptcy, not that long ago. This story should serve as an inspiration to other cities and to musicians in orchestras that might be facing difficulties.

It seemed so appropriate that this ICSOM conference, a meeting that would be marked by a new enthusiasm for the organization and a new optimism for orchestral music and the arts in America, would be held in this city where its orchestra has experienced such a magnificent rebirth. There is compelling evidence that orchestras are thriving, and there are beautiful new concert halls opening from Los Angeles to Raleigh and everywhere between.

But, there is always concern where orchestras are struggling, and where communities have failed to recognize the cultural, educational, and financial value of their orchestras. We would ask the citizens of such places why have they missed this opportunity? We would suggest that their mayors go to Nashville to see for themselves this opportunity to bring their cities, their constituents, and the business leaders of their state an unprecedented success. Let them see first-hand what such an investment from the business community of their cities can do for their citizens whom they have pledged to serve.

This Governing Board of ICSOM is inspired by the enthusiasm we observed in Nashville. We are energized by the collective wisdom of the delegates from your orchestras, and we are certain of our mission. ICSOM must re-engage our membership so that we can become the most visible and vocal advocate of symphony orchestras throughout America, and beyond.

As I assume my new position as chair of this historic organization, I am moved by the trust that has been placed in me, and I am acutely aware of what we all can learn from the lessons of the past. I am even more mindful of what the musicians of the future can learn from the message that we will now work to communicate in the most politically astute way possible. The arts and symphonic music in America must continue to grow and thrive. In cities where there are successes, that growth must be sustained. For cities that have failed to recognize this opportunity, we must demonstrate the value of a re-investment in their orchestra.

In my address to the delegates in Nashville, I borrowed a sentence that President Kennedy once used to inspire this nation. He said, "While we cannot guarantee that we shall one day be first, we can guarantee that any failure to make this effort will make us last."

This ICSOM Governing Board looks to you all for guidance, assistance, and support as we seek to spread the lessons we learned in Nashville.

Breaking the Fourth Wall

SENZA SORDINO
MARCH, 2007

I still remember vividly the first time I heard the Boston Symphony in a live concert, a 1978 performance of Schubert's C Major Symphony with Sir Colin Davis. For many years, I have had a book about that great orchestra called *Community of Sound,* by Louis Snyder. Twenty-seven years after its publication, it is enjoyable to read about a few of my teachers when they were younger and to see pictures of mentors sadly now absent. Of course, when I bought the book I was much younger too, which is a fact I find slightly less enjoyable. I've kept my copy for all of this time, and I've always especially liked its title. I've thought a great deal over the years about the phrase "community of sound." What does that really mean, and what could it come to mean in its full potential?

"Community" is a bit of a buzz word in the orchestra world today. I use it all the time. It appears more and more in the literature that surrounds the field, but I wonder if we are all using the word with the same meaning. We must strive to make sure that "community" refers not only to an investment in us, but that it also means that musicians invest in the community. To establish indelibly the positive sense of community that our Players' Associations seek to develop, musicians must learn to break the fourth wall.

In theater, the fourth wall is the imaginary wall between the stage and the audience, the other three walls being formed by the shell of the stage. In strictest terms it is the defining line between fiction and reality, or "the suspension of disbelief." In his theory of epic theater, Bertolt Brecht created the term "breaking the fourth wall" for that moment

11

when a character will turn, most uncharacteristically, to address the audience directly, thus giving the audience an access through reality to the fictional world they are observing on the stage. The term has been adapted from the theater to include books, film, and television.

Musicians in symphony orchestras can adapt the term to serve a new purpose as well. All too often in our concerts halls there seems to be a dividing line between the orchestra and the audience. To establish a closer relationship with our audiences, boards, and community leaders, orchestra musicians need to break the fourth wall.

I realize that I am distorting the term somewhat. In music, there is not the dramatic line between reality and fiction, though I suppose some would argue that point. But, allowing for that distinction and the adaptation, what would it mean for symphony musicians to break the fourth wall?

It would mean establishing a connection with the audience and inviting them into the community that surrounds every orchestra. Further, it would entail expanding that community to all constituents of the city or region.

How is such a thing accomplished? Sometimes the smallest gestures are the most appreciated and have the longest impact. On your players' association letterhead, you should send notes of thanks to reporters when they have written positive stories, to business leaders when they have made positive contributions, and to audiences members who have made special gestures of support. Send signed cards from the orchestra to your friends and supporters, marking those major life events that affect us all, whether happy, sad, or worrisome. While the signing of a card will take each of us mere seconds, some of these cards will hang on the walls of your biggest donors for years and live in their memories for decades.

Before the concert, walk through the lobby and shake a few hands. That's how you start to build relationships—simply by meeting people. In the sports world, it is said that the incredible (and to me, mystifying) rise of NASCAR is largely due to the accessibility of the participants to their fans. While it might be hard for us to imagine, an audience member's experience is greatly enhanced by a few words with the performers. That person will tell their friends, all of whom will remember the positive experience of their encounter with a member of the orchestra. In all walks of life, the more friends you have, the more support you have when it is needed.

How does all of this serve to ensure the survival of our institutions and the elevation of the livelihood of the orchestral performer?

The more our boards know about us, the more they will understand our lives and the inherent difficulties and challenges involved in making a living by performing in a symphony orchestra.

The more contact we have with our local press, the more trust we build. Through that connection, the positive message of our players' associations can be spread throughout the community.

The more access we create to our local political and business leaders, the greater our chance to communicate the financial role that our orchestras play in the healthy life of any city.

While these are indeed contacts that might be needed in times of crisis, they are also contacts that can be built to avoid such crises.

Some might correctly ask "Isn't it our management's job to promote a healthy image of the orchestra?" And the answer would most certainly be "Yes, it is." Where managements are advocating their orchestras with a positive message, then players' associations and ICSOM should be there to assist them. But in this era of negative rhetoric about the arts, there are many situations in which we must become our own advocates. We can no longer cede the pronouncement of a negative future for the arts in America.

I have heard of stories where some managers try to create the illusion of breaking the fourth wall by instructing their musicians to "smile more." The very idea of that directive assumes that the appearance of a happy workplace is more important that actually having a happy workplace. If you want the musicians to appear to be happy, isn't it apparent that creating a positive atmosphere would prove more effective than issuing a memo?

The turnover in managerial positions will almost always be greater than the turnover in your board and players' association. The musicians and the board can create an atmosphere that can sustain our organizations through the debates of our differences and lead us to the path of our shared visions for all that our orchestras can achieve.

All of our players' associations have any number of committees:

orchestra committees, negotiating committees, media committees, etc. It might be time for us all to invent another committee from within our ranks. This committee could be charged with fostering the environment of "family" that we all should hope will surround our orchestras. They could send cards to our members when they need the support of their colleagues. They could seek out opportunities to make gestures of friendship that would not only serve to unify us within our own orchestras, but also build positive relationships with those who surround and support our musicians in their city. So the next time you have an opportunity to elect your travel committee or artistic committee, I hope that we all will also consider electing a "community committee" that will serve to strengthen the orchestra within the bargaining unit and elevate the profile of the players' association in the minds of those we seek to serve.

At your next concert, imagine the fourth wall. Do you feel separated from your audiences? Sometime I sit back and wonder, "Why have these people left the safety of their homes to come and watch me work?" That's always an issue for musicians, isn't it? Is anybody really listening? Do our audiences fully understand what we are trying to do? Really, why are they there?

I suppose they've arrived in our concert halls for many reasons. Certainly, some have come merely to be seen, and some have been dragged by their dates. But those are the few. The vast and not so silent majority have come to listen, learn, remember, dream, and imagine. They have come to experience a convocation in their city. I see no "graying audience". I see a gathering of young and old who have come to see where we can take them.

In a time when every person's day is filled with its own unique difficulties, and in a world that slumps with its heavy burdens, they have come to allow their orchestra to provide them a moment for the suspension of their disbelief, a respite from the weight of their own day. That moment will serve as a reminder that the aspiration of the arts is the elevation of the human spirit.

For so long, the public has read of a decline in the relevance of the arts. But those questions of sustainability have been answered time and time again through the community service of the musicians in our orchestras and of those who support us. A recent report from the National

Endowment for the Arts concluded that 51% of people who regularly attend arts events were also volunteers that served their communities, while only 19% of non-attendees were so inclined. I'm afraid that some of the negative rhetoric about the future of the arts in America has left some members of the public with the view that artists feel a sense of entitlement, as if society owes us something. But the truth is society doesn't owe it to us to support the arts; society owes it to itself.

Let us now resolve to reach out to our public and our communities anew, by breaking the fourth wall.

Travels Without Charley

SENZA SORDINO
MAY, 2007

A few late-nights ago, with the help of a mileage calculating website, I added up my travels for ICSOM and other orchestral industry activities over the past fifteen months or so. I was only slightly surprised when I finished the math to see that I had flown over 40,000 miles during that span. I have met with musicians across the country, addressed young people entering the arts management field, visited with our friends in ROPA, OCSM, RMA, and TMA, toured concert halls, and heard rehearsals from San Juan to Honolulu—not to mention the many fine patty-melts I have enjoyed at airport diners.

I feel that I am gaining a unique picture of orchestras in America. I am meeting with musicians and their leadership in our orchestras. I am listening to rehearsals and attending concerts. I am backstage in the musicians' lounges, and visiting them in their homes. I am meeting their board members and their executive directors. My visits in all of these cities are far too brief, but I do get a wide-angle snapshot of these organizations that has served to educate me in a profound way about our musicians' lives and the great potential of our orchestras to serve their communities.

During these past fifteen months, I have heard the New York Philharmonic rehearsing in an empty Avery Fisher Hall and returned for a magnificent performance there. I heard the Puerto Rico Symphony in their rehearsal hall, and the San Antonio Symphony onstage at the visually amazing Majestic Theater. I have met with the Virginia Symphony in a giant dressing room at Chrysler Hall (the first place I ever heard a live orchestra), and the Charlotte Symphony onstage at the Blumenthal Center.

I have had the honor of speaking with the musicians of the Honolulu Symphony at their union hall, the legendary Local 677, when the vast majority of the orchestra spent close to five hours visiting with AFM Negotiator Nathan Kahn and me on their day off. I toured the concerts halls of the Los Angeles Philharmonic and the Nashville Symphony. As I write this, I will soon be listening to the Cleveland Orchestra and meeting with the Jacksonville Symphony and the Oregon Symphony.

I am learning enough to fill several volumes. At the risk of putting a viral tune in your head, I've learned primarily that it truly is a small world after all. For while every orchestra I visit faces some unique issue, many of our issues are the same. Far too often our musicians have come to believe the negative rhetoric about the future of the arts in America, and they need to hear a message that compels them to unite and believe in themselves. They need to hear that through ICSOM and their union, they can be a part of something greater than any individual.

Our orchestras all face some dispute within their own ranks, disputes that can only be addressed through the highest tone of debate and open democracy. But, all too often, they also face a board that is dealing with the very same issues. These problems, with their unavoidable fatigue and discouragement, tend to create a culture of hostility within our industry. This hostility sometimes inhibits our ability to communicate with our boards and our managements. It bears poison fruit in the press that perpetuates a negative future. Worst of all, it contaminates our ability to communicate among our ranks as a supportive bargaining and artistic unit.

There is nothing wrong with dissension, as long as it is expressed in a respectful environment. We are all performers, which means that something inside must convince us that we can command the attention of thousands of people on stage every night. Only strong-willed people who believe in themselves can pull off such a feat. It is only natural that self-assured people will occasionally need to debate their differences. That is the essence of the human and artistic experience. It is healthy, and the churning of emotion is how great art is made.

What I hear everywhere I go are incredible musicians performing at an absolutely astonishing level, no matter the size of the budget of their organization. The musicians I meet are inspired and inspiring people dedicated to serving their communities at the highest cultural level.

We must not let our souls fall victim to the culture of hostility. We have the ability to change all of that. And, most notably, we have the ability to put out a true and positive message about just what it is that our orchestras can do for our communities.

Here is a fact about the future of classical music: Last year, the genre of music that saw the greatest increase in downloads, an increase of over 22%, was classical music! That's right—the rumors of the death of our chosen art form have been greatly exaggerated.

I write often of my early years as a musician, where I was playing all kinds of music in all kinds of settings, some glorious and some unsavory. I was surrounded by mentors. There were sane and mundane people, crazy and brilliant people, and they all offered me an education into the world of music. I listened and I learned; and I heard all kinds of music imaginable.

But there was something else I first heard back then: the myth of the graying audience. I was told, back in 1979 when I started, that the audience for classical music would soon be dead.

And yet, when I look out at audiences today, I see the same faces I saw then. I see the young and the old, the well dressed and the sartorially challenged. I was thrilled on a recent visit to Avery Fisher Hall to see the youth that dominated the lobby at a New York Philharmonic concert. It made me feel a bit old! I left the concert that evening and wandered the streets of Manhattan, pondering how we might change the concert experience to ensure that symphonic music continues to appeal to the older generation.

The playwright Eugene Ionesco wrote: "A work is not a series of answers, it is a series of questions…it is not the answer that enlightens, but the question." Maybe that is what I have learned in my travels. Maybe it isn't the answer that is as important as the question. I'm reminded of that Harry Chapin song, where he sang "It's got to be the going, not the getting there, that's good."

We must remember that this we did with our lives for a reason. I read a great article in a Victoria, Canada, newspaper recently in which there was this quote: "A civilization is not judged by its ability to generate income."

It is our job as artists to remember that. We must rely on our managements to present the other truth, the real truth, that, in fact, the arts do indeed generate income for everyone in a community. Where our managers are not promoting that message, we must point out the tremendous opportunity presented to them by just how impressive our musicians are, both as artists and as human beings. The good managers will hear our message and thrive. The others will fail. This we assert without hesitation: it is a new day for symphonic music in America. ICSOM is spreading a different message. It is a message of hope. It is a message of the most profound community service.

Over 40,000 miles have I traveled, and over 40 years has ICSOM persevered. But, we've barely begun. Opportunity awaits, and the message must be spread. When I grow weary, I am comforted by the knowledge that there is a generation of friends performing on the same night, at the same moment, as I. There are mentors that went before me, and generations that will follow.

As the *New York Times* reported just last year, this can be classical music's golden age. In a world that is weary with conflict and hostility, we can serve as a beacon, a beacon that has every opportunity to grow brighter with every note we play, and through every life we touch. Some of the orchestras I have visited have generously said that ICSOM's presence has been inspirational. But, to those orchestras, I would say that ICSOM, and I, owe them our thanks. I have been inspired by every musician I've met and every orchestra I've heard. We exist because of our members, and, on all-night flights back to North Carolina, I am never alone. I hear their music, and I carry the strength of our community of musicians with me everywhere I go.

A Thousand Candles

SENZA SORDINO
OCTOBER, 2007

I've been thinking of this adage I once read in a book of quotations attributed to Buddha:

> "Thousands of candles can be lit from a single candle, and
> the life of the candle will not be shortened. Happiness
> never decreases by being shared."

My travels this summer to the AFM Convention and the conferences of ROPA, OCSM, and ICSOM have served to remind me of my earliest teachers and my union mentors. Though some are now absent, they all still hang around my consciousness. These were great people who lit thousands of candles, and in doing so became brilliant figures in my life.

My life would most certainly have been different without them. They opened my mind, not only to all kinds of music, but also to all kinds of people and ideas. They told me of the union, and they made it seem like an inviting and accepting place; a place where a move against one of us was a move against all of us. I wonder if my first encounters with the union had been negative, would I feel as strongly as I do about our network of friends and our community of musicians?

Among our students, what do we want their introduction to ICSOM and the union to be? Twenty-five years from now, the person who leads the union and the symphonic field might be one of your current students. Are they getting all of the messages they will need? Are they hearing a positive view of what solidarity can mean, or are they getting a different message?

We must give them a positive introduction. Teach them to respect their colleagues. Teach them not to criticize each other. It is a lesson that will serve us all to remember. As musicians, it is in our nature to be highly critical, even to ourselves. We are trained to analyze, criticize, and agonize over every note. We know instinctively that our reputations are only as good as the last note we have played.

Still, we can be more supportive of our colleagues. We can commend them for great performances, and we can support them in hardships. In a time of trouble (be it institutional or personal), our united network of friends can rise to their need.

So, you might ask, what is this really about? Am I actually spending a column of ink advocating that we be nice to each other?

While there are worse things to advocate, that's not at all why I'm writing this. I've told you all that just so I could tell you this: At one moment during my travels this summer, I heard a presentation about the union that was loud, ugly, threatening, and uninviting. At that moment, I thought that if this had been my introduction to the union, I never would have joined.

Instead, though, great mentors told me of ICSOM and the AFM. They regaled me with the legendary stories that we all share throughout the field. They spoke of solidarity, and were encouraging and supporting at every difficult moment I faced.

And that's why I'm writing all of this. What kind of mentoring will the next generation of orchestral musicians receive?

The 2007 ICSOM Conference in Minneapolis was an inspiring gathering for me and for your Governing Board. Amongst our delegates there was an exchange of ideas and enthusiasm, all in an atmosphere of inclusion and solidarity.

After my return home, I was pleased to read a report on the conference by Barbara Owens, President of Local 9-535 in Boston, who wrote that the "friendly tone of the conference was in sharp contrast to the tension of the recent AFM Convention" and that she was "grateful to be part of a process that was respectful and productive."

That "respectful and productive" tone, as well as the enthusiasm of your delegates, has invigorated us all for the tasks ahead. And there can be no doubt that these tasks are many. This season, many of our colleagues will face negotiations and we all will face the continuing negative rhetoric that inhibits the growth of our great institutions. But we left Minneapolis prepared to spread a positive message, prepared to stand united with every orchestra through whatever difficulty they may face, and prepared to work for unity throughout our union.

We are at an important time in the history of ICSOM, and indeed the history of the Union. While other segments of the union might be at odds, there is a great coming together within ICSOM, and we implore everyone to hear our calls for unity.

The work ahead is daunting, but we will succeed by reaching out to our colleagues, both within our own orchestra and throughout our community of friends across North America. We will communicate in richer ways, spreading stories of our successes and cautionary tales of our disappointments. There shall be many more of the former than the latter if we all truly work together. Invest in your orchestra, invest in your community, invest in ICSOM, and invest in the future by introducing your students to our positive message.

As our music reaches thousands in our community, our musicians reach an even greater number. We teach young people about music, and we lighten the burden of life for so many through the elevation of the human spirit.

The message our students and our audiences receive is up to us. It is up to each one of us to become a little more brilliant and light a few candles. We will only grow stronger through sharing that light.

Generational Shift

SENZA SORDINO
JUNE, 2008

The North Carolina Symphony recently performed an unusual concert, the brainchild of our music director, Grant Llewellyn. Maestro Llewellyn wanted our audiences to experience some of the musicians' other unique talents, besides the ones they are known for week in and week out. My talented colleagues were given the chance to perform in activities as disparate as flamenco dancing and bluegrass jamming. Our audiences loved every second.

As I enjoyed the concerts from the bass section, I was especially impressed by the bluegrass band that had been assembled. They were fantastic, and over four nights they truly brought down the house.

That band, known humorously as *Jackie and the Backstage Boys* (a nod to one of our orchestra's young stars, Jackie Saed Wolborsky, and the members of the stage crew that joined in on mandolin and guitar), was composed of members of the NCS with tenures ranging from over 35 years to less than eight months. As great as they were musically, I think I enjoyed the diversity in tenures as much as anything. Musicians who had been in the orchestra since before some of the others were born were performing together perfectly and with a camaraderie that demonstrated that this orchestra is truly a family. The embrace of our loyal audiences served to confirm even more the strength of the community that surrounds this orchestra.

I often consider how rare it is in today's world to find true loyalty. But throughout ICSOM, we have musicians who have dedicated their entire lives to their orchestra, and to serving their community and educating its children.

Every orchestra has a unique sound, a product of the individuals who have developed that sound over time. It is a mix if the young and the more experienced. I find myself reinvigorated by that relationship, both in my own orchestra and as I observe it in others.

Our orchestras and indeed our communities are enriched by our diversity. I have seen how the newer members seek to learn from the history of the orchestra, and how we all can be invigorated by youth.

Every person is in a period of transition every day of their lives. When I joined the North Carolina Symphony, I was the youngest member at the time. I have now lost that distinction—by several decades no less. How can it be true?

Occasionally, we will hear a manager or music director talking about "generational shift." That would be fine if they were speaking of the natural process of time, but we know they aren't. There are some who fail to appreciate how our orchestras are strengthened by the diversity of experience on stage. Fortunately, the federal government does appreciate it, as demonstrated through the enactment of The Age Discrimination in Employment Act of 1967.

My friends in my orchestra have served this state through changing times and decades, and long before we had a world-class concert hall in Raleigh. My more tenured colleagues were pioneers, bringing music to school children throughout the state on old buses and rural back roads. While the accommodations and the highways have improved immeasurably, education remains a critical part of our mission. The trail blazers that arrived before me created an identity for this orchestra, and they bought the AFM to its members, fighting tirelessly for many years to achieve a pension, health care, and many other benefits that are today simply expected.

The same is true for orchestras throughout ICSOM, and the biographies of our members consistently tell the story of hard fought battles and victories slowly won amidst an atmosphere of incredible loyalty and ongoing artistic accomplishment.

As I watched my colleagues perform together and observed the sense of ownership our audiences feel, I couldn't help but think of the musicians of the Columbus Symphony (CSO). Indeed, they've not been far from my mind at any moment during these past few months. I was impressed with Barbara Zuck's May 11 review of the CSO in the *Columbus Dispatch* in which she points out that the popularity of the orchestra is rising at the very moment that the board threatens to lockout the musicians and damage the community's investment in that orchestral family.

I couldn't help but contrast two recent editorials, one from Raleigh's *News and Observer*, and the other from the *Columbus Dispatch*. Here in North Carolina we are fortunate to have a great newspaper that seeks to serve its state, and they support the musicians at every turn. Throughout this recent crisis in Columbus, the citizens have not been able to rely on the *Columbus Dispatch* to serve their community in the same way.

In response to a new outreach program the NCS has initiated, the editorial staff of the *News and Observer* wrote:

> *"Ever since its formation in 1932, the N.C. Symphony has belonged to the people...Here is an appropriate gesture of solidarity from this grand group of musicians to the citizens who have long supported the orchestra. ...OK, OK, we know this isn't a miracle working tour. Or is it?"*

Compare that to the words of the editorial staff of the *Columbus Dispatch*, just a few days later, when speaking of the musicians of the CSO.

> *"The union disingenuously accuses the board of being derelict in its duty to seek out more donations...The musicians should stop focusing on blame and start dealing with the facts...The Columbus Symphony Orchestra is at a crossroads that will determine whether it continues or folds. The outcome is in the hands of the musicians union."*

Can there be any doubt that the citizens of central Ohio deserve better from their hometown newspaper?

I imagine that I am now past the midway point of my career. I remember the beginning, with the Virginia Symphony Orchestra, as if I could still somehow touch it. I remember the scent of backstage—I could name every musician on stage with me that night in February of 1979. We played Brahms' First Symphony in Norfolk's Chrysler Hall. After the show I had a barbeque sandwich and a limeade at Doumars' drive-in and wondered what the future would bring. Little did I know...

To my more tenured colleagues across the nation, I urge you to be invigorated by our newest members, and to help them understand the battles that you have fought. To our newest members, I urge you to be inspired by your colleagues, and to realize that it will seem like a very brief time before you also find yourself standing at your midway point. And to any manager that speaks of any need for a "generational shift" in their orchestra, I urge them to think about music (and life) in a richer way.

Civil Discourse

SENZA SORDINO
AUGUST, 2008

I have been thinking a great deal recently about the importance of civil discourse. A few years back I wrote about what I perceived as a "culture of hostility" in our field. I meant this to include both the relationships between musicians and managers, as well as the relationships among musicians themselves. Every season we elect some of our colleagues to endure a most onerous task, that of serving on the orchestra committee, and then we all too frequently reward their offer of volunteer service with abuse instead of support.

Of course, the democratic process that we all embrace should welcome an avenue for disagreements and respectful debate. But all too often these disagreements are expressed in the form of personal attacks and name calling. We are all the weaker as a result.

Throughout my work in these past two years as chair of ICSOM, time and time again I have received calls from committee chairs who are facing personal criticism as they try to serve. I always counsel them with the advice that if everybody liked you, it would probably mean that you were doing something wrong.

One of my teachers told me many years ago, "If you are going to stand for anything in this world, there will be people who will stand against you. Some will oppose you because of what you stand for, and others will oppose you simply because you are able to stand."

As I look out across the ICSOM landscape, I see great reason for hope, and I feel an uplifting optimism. Every time we have asked our member orchestras to act as a unified body, they have done so. Through uniting, and through seeking a richer dialogue, we can defeat the culture of hostility. Our organization is strong enough to welcome disagreement, provided that we also decide not to tolerate personal attacks.

The strengthening of the unity within ICSOM offers great hope for this union, its members, and musicians everywhere. But our unity must be nurtured. We are not without our problems.

Perhaps the most potentially divisive area that symphonic musicians face is in the area of media. There is a great disparity of opinion, and these opinions are quite strongly held. As many have observed, it is interesting that media would be the source of division within the symphonic ranks, since it produces just a small amount of our income. But, it is vitally important to our future, and we will have to engage in debate as new technologies offer new opportunities. It is equally important for us to work to preserve fair compensation for the highly skilled labor we perform, especially when that labor is even more difficult to perform with a microphone and camera two inches from your bell, bow or brow.

Despite these concerns I feel the sense of community is growing among our orchestras. That strength is entirely due to the musicians who perform nightly, and their elected committee leaders who voluntarily surrender time with their families to serve all of us.

In this year, I have been inspired by the dedication and altruistic service of our musician leaders across the country. I have been moved by the overwhelming response of our orchestras to their colleagues in need. While others might be mired in dissension, ICSOM aspires to a greater goal. I hope that we have only just begun to accomplish even greater things for our field. But to do that, we must reject the culture of hostility. We must continue to elevate the tone of our debates, and we must always strive to avoid expressing our disagreements through personal attacks.

Now More Than Ever

SENZA SORDINO
APRIL, 2009

> *"I see little of more importance to the future of our country and our civilization than full recognition of the place of the artist. I look forward to an America which will reward achievement in the arts as we reward achievement in business or statecraft. I look forward to an America which will steadily raise the standards of artistic accomplishment and which will steadily enlarge cultural opportunities for all of our citizens."*
> —*John F. Kennedy, October 26, 1963*

On January 20, 2009, all of America celebrated some of the nation's greatest instrumentalists when Yo-Yo Ma, Itzhak Perlman, Anthony McGill and Gabriela Montero performed immediately prior to President Obama's oath of office. I was privileged to be standing backstage at Orchestra Hall in Minneapolis, watching the historic event with the musicians of the Minnesota Orchestra. Regardless of political ideology, all Americans could feel pride in celebrating the great tradition of the arts in this country, as represented by some of the greatest musicians of the century.

But less than 20 days after that inspirational moment, the music almost died in Congress.

There can be no doubt that America faces a recession the likes of which most of us have never seen in our lifetimes. As Washington pondered how best to construct a stimulus to our nation's economy, huge numbers like $800 or $900 billion were discussed as if we could possibly comprehend them. Now, as of the Senate's final action on the package, it is set at $783 billion.

Of that huge number, I saw no appropriation attacked as vigorously as the $50 million that was destined for the National Endowment for the Arts (NEA). In fact, an amendment proposed by Senator Tom Coburn (R-OK) was adopted. The Coburn amendment excluded use of stimulus dollars for "museums, art centers, and theaters." In proposing this egregious amendment, Senator Coburn somehow masterfully (or should I say artlessly) tied funding for the arts to "gambling establishments."

Through the efforts of artists across the country, over 85,000 letters were delivered to members of Congress urging them to restore funding for the arts to the stimulus package. Thousands of these letters came from symphonic musicians who responded to ICSOM's appeal to work together through our partnership with Americans for the Arts (AFTA). The advocacy and the activism worked. The Colburn amendment was repealed and the $50 million for the NEA was restored.

As Congress seeks to reinvigorate our economy, I couldn't agree more that we must analyze the value of every dollar spent. And one of the best possible investments for our dollars is in the arts. According to AFTA, the $50 million in the House version of the economic stimulus package could save well over 14,000 American jobs.

If it is possible to accurately calculate the math on such huge figures, the $50 million that can save these jobs is about 0.006% of the stimulus package. And yet, from media accounts, you would think that the arts are antithetical to the economic recovery, as opposed to a vital component.

The *National Review* wrote: "The National Endowment for the Arts is in line for $50 million. The unemployed can fill their days attending abstract-film festivals and sitar concerts."

This statement of course astonishingly ignores the fact that 5.7 million jobs are provided by the arts. And really—sitar concerts was the best they could come up with?

Representative Jack Kingston (R-GA) said in the *Congressional Quarterly*: "I just think putting people to work is more important than putting more art on the wall of some New York City gallery frequented by the elite art community. Call me a sucker for the working man."

Whether or not Rep. Kingston happens to be a sucker, I will suggest that he is terribly misinformed and is merely repeating the tired talking points provided by pundits from over two decades ago.

The press was quick to add nothing to the debate, aside from ill-informed stereotypes.

> *"True to form, Congress has loaded the [bill] with hundreds of billions in wasteful spending. The bill includes $650 million for digital TV coupons, $140 million to study the atmosphere and $50 million for the National Endowment for the Arts. None of these proposals would create jobs or boost our economy. They're just old-fashioned waste"*
>
> —Op-ed in the *Indianapolis Star*

> *"The National Endowment for the Arts would get $50 million for new exhibits to deem America racist and sexist."*
>
> —Op-ed in the *Norwich Bulletin*

The arts in America are a tremendous investment, providing an almost unprecedented return. Every dollar that the government invests in the arts returns seven dollars to the community. The $50 million that Senator Coburn attempted to rip from the stimulus package has the potential to return $350 million to the nation's economy. What other elements of the package offer such potential for the value of the taxpayer's hard earned dollar?

Here is what the arts mean for the economy of our nation each year:

- $104.2 billion in household income
- $7.9 billion in local government tax revenues
- $9.1 billion in state government tax revenues
- $12.6 billion in federal income tax revenues

It is easy for Senator Coburn and the *National Review* to repeat unchallenged rhetoric from the 1980s about NEA funding of specific projects. But their constituents, and the entire nation, deserve better at this time of economic crisis.

Whether you support the entire stimulus package or not, wouldn't you like to see a return of 7 to 1 on your tax dollar? An investment in the arts is just that—an investment with tangible returns. The money proposed for the arts will mean jobs for our communities, and will be invigorating for the cities where our children learn, our citizens live, and our companies do business.

There have been several examples of late that testify to the value and effectiveness of the activism of musicians. A petition created by ICSOM musician Jaime Austria (New York City Opera) calling for the creation of a Secretary for the Arts has inspired over 240,000 signatures. And then there are the 85,000 letters to Congress. Out of this bleak economic moment in our country's history, a new era of activism can and must arise through the spirit of unity among ICSOM and our friends.

We must not be dissuaded by hard times. Instead we must be inspired to voice our beliefs even more clearly, and we must be driven to unite and advocate for our communities.

A few years ago, it seemed to me that the arts were losing the argument of economics. ICSOM sought out a path to increase awareness of the importance of the arts and our orchestras to the financial health of our country. Along the way, we have found a few allies, and won a few victories.

But as I watched Mr. Ma and Mr. Perlman at the inaugural performance, I was struck by the spiritual importance of the moment. It had been a very long time since I had seen classical instrumentalists given such a prestigious honor as to take center stage at the historic moment of a presidential inauguration. It now seems to me that we have an opportunity to explore a new series of opportunities for the arts in America, and in doing so we must not emphasize only the economic argument to the exclusion of the cultural value of our orchestras. I once quoted a long lost newspaper article that eloquently reminded us that "a civilization is not judged by its ability to generate income."

Recently, in preparing for a guest teaching appearance at the Colburn School in Los Angeles, I reviewed my remarks to the Federation International des Musiciens in Berlin last year. Some of these words have appeared in these pages before, but at this time of difficulties, I feel compelled to repeat them.

"Everywhere we look there is evidence of the power of symphonic music. It

is seen and heard through historical events. It was experienced internationally when Leonard Bernstein conducted Beethoven's Ninth Symphony here in this great city at the fallen Berlin Wall. It is heard on one of my favorite vinyl records; an amazing live recording by the Boston Symphony of Mozart's Requiem at a memorial mass for President Kennedy in January of 1964. I felt it on the lawn at Duke University immediately following the terrorist attacks of September 11, where thousands of people held candles as they listened reverently to their own symphony orchestra, a scene repeated throughout the world by hundreds of orchestras in hundreds of locations. It is felt in the response of our audiences and seen throughout our communities as we help attract businesses, educate our children, and spread the name of our great cities.

We must remember... this we did with our lives for a reason. While it is and has always been so in vogue for orchestral musicians to be cynical, it is not beyond us to continue to indulge in our dreams. The greatest musicians among us are those who are still inspired by the opportunity to inspire. Through uniting together and reaching out to our communities, we can and will ensure that the arts continue to thrive, and we will continue to enrich the lives of our audiences as we improve the livelihood of our colleagues, all while inspiring the next generation of musicians.

Let our community of musicians serve as an example to those places across the globe that are aching to hear a positive message.

It is a right of the people that they not be deprived of hope. As they hear our music, let them also hear our voices.

We are the advocates for our art form, we are the advocates for our communities, and we are the advocates for our children. Through our music, we offer a message of hope that the world is longing to hear."

Let us not falter in our mission. Let us not be discouraged, but instead let us be inspired to greater activism by the recent successes. As the economy faces the prospect of getting worse before it gets better, we all must be engaged in advocacy for our art form, for our communities, and for our friends. We must not allow hard times to impair our idealism.

I do not doubt that we will weather this crisis, because I have faith in the musicians of ICSOM, and I have been inspired by the unity we have demonstrated. Soon there will be even more opportunities for activism... within our communities, and within our union.

I know we all will respond.

The New Apocalypticism

SENZA SORDINO
JULY, 2009

The economic conditions that have led us to a year of crisis for orchestras in America have also spawned a new phrase for the rhetoric about our field: "The New Economic Reality".

I have to confess that I don't really have any idea what that means. I don't mean to be obtuse—clearly I know what those who use that phrase are talking about. But we are in a recession, and I'm not sure what's so new about that. While this is possibly the worst recession of our lifetimes, it has nonetheless happened before, and many times at that. Recessions have always been followed by a recovery, and this one will be as well.

In 1958, the United States found itself mired in a deep recession. Sales of automobiles that year fell 31%, and unemployment in Detroit stood at 20% (a comparable figure to 2009). There was a debate within the Eisenhower administration about the budget, with the President insisting on a balanced budget from the Congress, and with Vice-President Nixon concerned that such a balanced budget could deepen the recession, leading to mid-term election losses and undermining his own campaign for the presidency in 1960. Eisenhower won out, the recession deepened, and Nixon lost the 1960 election, due in part to the economy (and also several thousand votes harvested from cemeteries on the outskirts of Chicago.) I've always thought the lesson of this was that in a recession, you don't balance your budget, but you manage your debt.

There are major differences between all of these past recessions and the one we face today. None of these differences are more profound than the omnipresence of the 24-hour news cycle. It seems that the only

34

industry that is truly thriving now is punditry, and the more outrageous the commentary, the more the pundit profits. There is no penalty for being wrong—or for being irresponsible. In fact, as long as it is outrageous and loud, the talking heads are rewarded. Isn't that the definition of a snake oil salesman? Someone who profits from the fear they promulgate.

In past times ideologues had to have their ideas assimilated into society, but today they have virtually uncensored, open platforms. There are cable news channels devoted to ideology, and websites galore that publish extremist views unchallenged. I've become unable to watch even those who profess to share my personal political ideology. None of these paid pundits are helping America. Instead, they merely preach a kind of apocalypticism in a culture where, if it bleeds, it leads. This pervasive negativity and bipolar debate permeates all of society, hindering recovery and casting a pall generated and spread by ratings.

Our field is no less immune than any other, and in some ways even more susceptible due to the negative perspective on the arts, and of the future of the arts, that we have long fought against. We must resist succumbing to this negativity as we ask ourselves how to best weather this storm.

In my view, "the new economic reality" is really just "the new apocalypticism."

I heard a story recently on NPR about Elkhart, Indiana, a town known as "The RV Capital of America." Apparently, very few people are buying recreational vehicles in the recession, and Elkhart's economy is in terrible shape. A resident of Elkhart wrote to NPR, saying that he wished the media would stop covering the situation in Elkhart as a convenient story of economic disaster. He likened it to the coverage of Allentown, when the steel mills shut down in the 1980's. He said that "all Allentown got out of it was a Billy Joel song." When we hear these stories, no one is thinking that Elkhart might be a bargain location to move a business, now with lower real estate costs and a ready work force. Instead, for the benefit of a political point, the town is portrayed as dead.

In this time of concern for the future of our orchestras, we must not allow a rhetoric of failure to negatively impact our recovery and the future of our orchestras. We must not allow a cyclical economic downturn to fundamentally alter the mission of artistry and community service our orchestras provide.

Musicians ultimately are the biggest donors to their own organizations. We are seeing that again when in this time of need our musicians are demonstrating incredible flexibility and dedication. We are adjusting our contracts, we are responding to "An" economic reality, even if it isn't a "New" economic reality. That catch phrase isn't required to get musicians' attention. We know what is happening. What employees would have done more? The musicians of the Honolulu Symphony have not been paid in 16 weeks, yet they continue to fight for the 110 year old orchestra with inspiring commitment.

In the negativity of the media, unions often are portrayed as inflexible. The debate has come up in the auto industry, where people wistfully point to non-union auto manufacturing in the south as an example that the union workers of Detroit should follow. The comparison boggles my mind.

These factory jobs were viewed as a way for Americans to march into the middle class, and that would never have been possible without the unions. Now, in this market, the unions of that industry have shown the flexibility that musicians have, and made adjustments needed to save their company. And while times have changed, industries have changed, and economies have changed, the negative view of the unions' role continues to roil.

When did it become a part of America that the worker should aspire to less?

Our musicians have a unique and intimate knowledge of their field, and we must work to share that education with our boards. Every crisis is also an opportunity, and in this time of economic crisis we must seek out the opportunity to share our knowledge with our boards so that together we can inspire our communities to invest in the growth of our orchestras. As I have often written, no "business" or other organization ever solved a financial problem by offering an inferior product to its consumers.

Even in this difficult time, we are seeing good managers leading their organizations to new eras of growth. We cannot allow others to use this economic downturn as an opportunity to reduce our greatest artistic and cultural organizations to a size that they find more manageable. Instead, we must find managers than can inspire boards and communities. In the absence of such leaders, the musicians themselves must be the advocates for their orchestras.

This recession will end. A recovery awaits. *The Wall Street Journal* recently predicted that the recession will end in September, but we must be wary of all punditry at this point. In fact, even if the recession does end soon, the lag effect on certain economic factors, such as unemployment, will remain. Our orchestras must be prepared to participate in the impending recovery. We can only achieve that by continuing with our positive message of hope, and by rededicating ourselves to the preservation of America's greatest cultural institutions.

This is no time to retreat. This is a time that calls for leadership, within our orchestras, within our communities, and within our union.

The Rubenstein Atrium
at Lincoln Center

SENZA SORDINO
APRIL, 2010

Performing arts centers can transform cities, enhancing the lives of citizens and the business environment. During a recent visit to New York City, I visited the new David Rubenstein Atrium at Lincoln Center, one of over 500 Privately Owned Public Spaces (POPS) in New York City created under a program that offers incentives for buildings to provide publicly accessible spaces in the community.

I received a tour of the Atrium, and also the beautifully renovated Koch Theater, from the New York City Opera's ICSOM delegate Gail Kruvand, and former delegate Nancy McAlhany. Later in the week I was also able to visit with the committee of the New York City Ballet and their delegate, Ethan Silverman, and greet some of the musicians in the renovated orchestra pit just prior to a Sunday matinee ballet performance.

There is a lot of renovation going on around Lincoln Center these days, and the Rubinstein Atrium truly impressed me. The Atrium is an example of how the arts community can enhance the living environment within any city.

The Rubenstein Atrium serves as the box office for all of the theaters at Lincoln Center, and for all twelve of the resident arts organizations. The Atrium is named in honor of Lincoln Center Vice Chairman David Rubinstein, and features (in addition to the box office) a fully staffed information desk, restrooms, free Wi-Fi, and a café with food from celebrity chef Tom Colicchio (of *Top Chef* fame). The beautifully designed area has two vertical gardens, a fountain, a wall designed for video presentations, and public art by Dutch textile artisan Claudy Jongstra.

I passed through this space a few times when it was known as the Harmony Atrium, but it was never fully utilized. Today, it is filled with people learning about the events at Lincoln Center, meeting with the artists, purchasing tickets, or awaiting same day discounts at the Donald and Barbara Zucker box office. The Atrium is open to the public 365 days a year until 10:00 pm, with the box office open until shortly before concert time. More information is available at the Lincoln Center website.

At a time when the relevancy of the arts continue to be under attack, I can think of many downtown areas that could benefit from such a convenient and inviting space near their Performing Arts Centers. When you visit such a creative area and see the innovative use of space within a city, it is tremendously inspiring.

While there is much consternation in the field over the release of the recent National Endowment for the Arts report that showed a drop in attendance for all art forms in America, the timing of the study makes me doubt the results. As Alex Ross said in the February 8, 2010 issue of *The New Yorker*: "Despite the dire trends, the classical audience remains reasonably healthy. Although a smaller portion of the population is heading out to concerts, those who do go are going more often: orchestras reported a slight rise in attendance between 2003 and 2007." I believe that innovative thinking, such as what led to the Rubenstein Atrium, will make it easier for our audiences to find us, and for new audiences to seek us out.

We must remember that the economic argument for the arts is central to our theme, accompanying the education and artistic message that our orchestras provide. In my home state of North Carolina, a recent study proclaimed that the creative industry in the state contributes $41 billion to the state's economy, and yet every time there is an appropriation for the arts, we have to read letters to the editor proclaiming it frivolous. By that same account, the wine industry in North Carolina, which is celebrated and encouraged, has an $813 million dollar impact. Of course, the wine industry is generally for-profit, and many of the agencies of the creative industry are non-profits. But, those creative industries account for 300,000 jobs, and the wine industry accounts for 5,700.

Please, don't get me wrong. The wine industry in our state is crucial to our economy, and we are proud to rank tenth in the nation in wine production. It should be supported and celebrated through every means possible, but the creative and artistic industries should also be recognized for what they truly provide. Instead, some critics react with the same old rhetoric, usually because the facts are so difficult to hear through the din of despair and hand-wringing that serves to undermine support for the arts.

Spaces like the Rubinstein Atrium demonstrate clearly what an investment in the arts can do for a community. Next time you are in New York City, I encourage you all to visit the Atrium, and take the message it represents back to your home cities as well as your local government, business, and arts leaders.

The Way Things Are is Not the Way Things Have to Be

SENZA SORDINO
JUNE, 2010

As I write this, I have begun my preparations for the 98th Convention of the American Federation of Musicians, to be held June 21-25, 2010, in Las Vegas. I will arrive with the hope that we will create a more unified union, but I will also arrive with trepidation that the atmosphere of internal fighting and negativity will persist.

I believe that the way things are is not the way things have to be.

The way things are:

1. A negative image of the future for the arts in America persists, despite evidence to the contrary that could be used to promote a future of growth.

2. Negotiating committees in orchestras around the country are weary from the constant threats from their managements of bankruptcy and force majeure, situations that are, in many cases, the result of managerial decisions and not just the economic downturn. Musicians are fearful, and managements are emboldened by our compliance.

3. Orchestral musicians turn to our union, a federation of locals, for support, but instead they are often met with political attacks and disregard. Musicians of all styles that would seek to band together are instead often torn apart by the politicization of our Federation and by a structure that seems to value discord over debate.

The way things could be:

1. An atmosphere of unity could be fostered within our union. Personal attacks could end. Dialogue and debate could be initiated. We could join together with a spirit of "what happens to one of us happens to all of us." Where disagreements exist, forums could be created for conversation and respectful debate.
2. The unity and communication within ICSOM could be a model for the entire union, promoting renewed strength and hope for Federation members.
3. ICSOM's positive message of hope for the future of the arts could be promoted by every member of this union. Communities across the country eager for a positive message could be invited to join our community of orchestras and musicians. The union could become a source of inspiration for our members, and the audiences and citizens we serve.

Recently, I have been reading a book by Miriam Pawel about the evolution of the United Farm Workers, titled *The Union of Their Dreams: Power, Hope, and Struggle in Cesar Chavez's Farm Worker Movement.* I love the title of this book. The brave founders of the UFW were creating the union of their dreams, and they did so by uniting their dreams.

I think maybe that is what has been lost in the American Federation of Musicians. Our dreams are no longer united. In fact, we seem at cross purposes almost everywhere we turn, as frequently the most basic issues are politicized and division is used as a political tool.

But the way things are is not the way things have to be. I believe that we all still share the same dreams. It has just become impossible to hear that shared idealism over the din of divisiveness, the personal attacks, the political maneuvering, and the lack of an inspirational message.

We all believe in a strong union that can serve its members. We all believe in the role that musicians can play in community service. We all believe in the value of our art. We all believe that we must educate the next generation. And, we all believe in the message of hope that our music and our work can provide.

But, in this fractured union, we are undermining our dreams. We are not harvesting from common ground but instead are sowing seeds of distrust that limit our ability to be true advocates for the arts in North America and across the world. This union could be a beacon for our dreams, but, instead, it is becoming a roadblock.

In recent years, the musicians of ICSOM have become more unified, even in troubled times. We have answered calls to action to assist our colleagues. A move against one of us is a move against all of us. In the nearly 50 years since ICSOM was created, the organization has served as an advocate for the arts and our members, and we have sought out opportunities to respectfully debate our differences while also uniting our dreams.

These opportunities can still be found in the AFM. It is not too late—but it is getting there. An inspirational message must arise from this 2010 Convention, or the future of our union could be very dark.

The way things are is not the way things have to be. We can create the union of our dreams.

The Uncertainty of Silence

SENZA SORDINO
DECEMBER, 2010

One of the most jarring juxtapositions in American film comes from *The Deer Hunter*, where lifelong friends spend one final night of celebration in a Pennsylvania mining town before they are sent to Vietnam. Arriving drunk and exhausted in their local hangout, Chopin's *Nocturne* No. 6 in G minor is played on an out-of-tune bar room piano, momentarily entrancing the friends just before an immediate cut to the sound of helicopters in war time. That scene never fails to take me by surprise, even though I am expecting it. I am struck by the ability of music to express so many beautiful and conflicting thoughts, while the lack of music is used to signify only uncertainty.

The symphonic music "industry" is so interesting. Our jobs are based upon recreating the most beautiful musical compositions in history, and recreating them as beautifully as possible. We spend our lives seeking to elevate the human spirit, and yet there are elements of our field that are, frankly, ugly. Recently, the uncertainty of silence has been felt in Detroit, and some of that ugliness emerged in the events that surrounded a possible recital there by Ms. Sarah Chang.

With the musicians of the Detroit Symphony Orchestra (DSO) on strike, the management of the DSO sought to convert a scheduled concerto appearance by Ms. Chang to a solo recital, unfortunately putting this great artist in the position of having to cross a picket line. It was, I'm sure, a terrible dilemma for her, and one from which her professional artist management agency should have protected her. Her management makes a great profit for protecting her interests, and in this case they clearly let her down. She became embroiled in an international event that she probably knew little about.

To make matters worse, when Ms. Chang ultimately canceled her recital, the management of the Detroit Symphony shamefully threw her under the proverbial bus, saying in the *New York Times* (October 12, 2010) that Ms. Chang "has crossed other picket lines."

Now, I honestly don't know if that statement is true or not, and neither does the *New York Times*. They just printed the accusation, without investigating to ever follow up. Scores of readers are left to assume that it is true, along with the accusations that Ms. Chang was "threatened" and that Ms. Chang's "cellphone number (was posted) on the web." But the *Times* did not require the DSO's management to produce proof of these statements, and readers across the world who saw the first part of the article on page C1 were no doubt left with the impression that union thugs had "viciously" threatened the young superstar until she felt "uncomfortable appearing in public."

Of course, if the reader were to turn the section of the paper all the way back to page C6, they would have read that the comments posted by musicians across the world "overwhelmingly used respectful or neutral language."

There is no doubt that some things were said that I found unfortunate. But, whenever anything is posted on the Internet, people writing anonymously as they sit in their underwear late at night will say some harsh things. Check out any article on-line about a baseball game, or a school board meeting, or for that matter a food bank drive and you may well see people writing mean-spirited things. It is, unfortunately, the side effect of an anonymous and instantaneous method of communication that gives us the ability to communicate instantly without saying anything at all. In 1992, Bob Dylan wrote "Technology to wipe out the truth is now available. Not everybody can afford it but it's available. When the cost comes down, look out!" Well, in 2010, the cost has clearly come down.

Truth be told, I am proud of the musicians who wrote to Ms. Chang. The story is not that a handful of people called her "scab" but that hundreds of people wrote in a respectful and courteous manner, praising her artistry, complimenting her career, and expressing admiration. But, I suppose that might not sell newspapers.

I have lost a lot of sleep over this incident. It seems to typify the worst of our field, where civility breaks down and leads to inaccurate journalism that certainly doesn't serve the cause of advocacy. I was interviewed for the *Times* article, but none of my statements appeared, save for a quote from my letter to Ms. Chang (a letter which, by the way, was sent to her management and not posted on her Facebook page, at least not by me.) When I told the reporter that I thought the appeals from musicians had been largely positive, I was told that I was engaging in spin, which was exactly what I had just said about the unfortunate accusations from the management of the DSO. Don't such accusations deserve follow up questions?

I was deeply disheartened to read the article the next day.

We can always improve—and we must improve. We can express ourselves in a way that will inspire our audiences and the next generation. No one is inspired by ugly language. I will admit that I am always saddened to read negative statements when we have so many positive ways to advocate our art and our communities. I wish no one had written "scab." While an historic term, it is an insult and I wish some had waited before tossing it around the internet. After all, ultimately she wasn't one. And yes, I did read "[expletive] Sarah Chang" on someone else's personal Facebook page. But that was an internal post, from a Facebook "friend" whom I have since "unfriended". I just can't afford that level of negativity in my life as I work to keep myself inspired to advocate for musicians everywhere.

Despite how this story was ultimately spun against musicians, I am proud of the elevated tone. And to Ms. Chang, I would like to offer my thanks and praise. I wish that your management had protected you from this situation, and I wish that the DSO management did not stain your reputation in the *New York Times*. If you were disturbed by troubling messages that I never saw, I regret that, and I understand. In fact, in the on-line exchange someone wrote a few nasty things about me too. It didn't feel great, but I understood that the person who attacked me does not know me, and apparently had not read my missive which I wrote so carefully to be respectful.

To use a phrase that seems to have become suddenly popular, I would hope that the field at large (musicians, orchestra managers, artist managements, and journalists) can use this event as a "teachable moment" and that we all can elevate our debates in the service of our communities and for future generations, before the negative false rhetoric permanently damages the beauty we all seek to recreate, and leads to the uncertainty of silence.

If you stand for anything in life, people will take shots at you. Some will attack you because of what you stand for, and some will attack you simply because you are able to stand. I choose to stand anyway. And on behalf of musicians everywhere, we thank Sarah Chang for standing with us on this occasion.

The Best of Times,
the Worst of Times

SENZA SORDINO
MARCH, 2011

Recently, Michael Steele (former head of the Republican National Committee) was asked to name his favorite book, and he answered *War and Peace*. He then went on to quote from the book, saying "It was the best of times; it was the worst of times." Aside from not knowing the difference between Tolstoy and Dickens, I thought his reference was appropriate, as it is the best of times, and it is the worst of times.

The notion that anything about these times might be positive must seem to be a fantastic statement when we look at the state of art and music in America. We are seeing a renewed series of attacks on the arts and attacks on unions. It feels like 1980 all over again. The air traffic controllers union was wiped out by the government, and opponents of public funding for the arts would soon attack the funding of one photographer as indicative of moral decay and federal waste.

Ahh, nostalgia. Leg warmers, anyone?

In 2011, legislators have once again proposed drastic cuts to the National Endowment for the Arts, and a few have suggested eliminating funding completely. This despite the fact that every dollar the government invests in the arts returns seven dollars to the community.

It is patently absurd to suggest that in order to address budget deficits, we must cut the NEA. The deficit is something like $1.5 trillion, and the budget for the NEA is $165 million. It is such a small fraction of the budget—a little over one one-hundredth of one percent—that cutting it in order to achieve fiscal responsibility is a little like gambling away all of your savings, and then deciding to unplug your microwave to save money on electricity. Our country needs to create jobs, and the arts lead to over 5.7 million jobs annually.

And what else is wrong? Well, where do I begin?

As of this writing, The Detroit Symphony remains on strike, with management having "suspended" the rest of the season. The musicians of the Louisville Orchestra had to resist an attempt by their management to put them into bankruptcy; fortunately, a judge refused to uphold this attempt. A renewed attack on unions has led to widespread demonstrations, most notably in Madison, Wisconsin, but also in town squares and government plazas across America.

It is the age of wisdom, and it is the age of foolishness

It might appear that there is not much good happening right now—but I don't see it that way.

I look out and sense that we are entering a renewed era of activism. Those who would seek to undermine the arts in America may well overplay their hand. Even politicians such as Mike Huckabee are fighting back against the negativity of denying our children access to the arts. The demonstrations in Madison have been uniformly civil and positive. In our field, while some managements seek to study their own demise and create "a new model" that would only hasten the erosion of our greatest cultural institutions, there are also other voices speaking out, and other successes being achieved despite what some see as a concerted attempt from the field to thwart the positive efforts. Michael Kaiser is traveling across the world with his positive message, and musicians are unifying in even greater ways. The musicians of the Cincinnati Symphony and the National Symphony have reached out to assist the Louisville Orchestra musicians (if I may call them that) in a tremendous show of friendship and support.

(I muse on whether I can mention the musicians of the Louisville Orchestra, as their management has absurdly prohibited them from using that name. To quote from the musicians' press release: "Major Orchestra Across Ohio River from Jeffersonville, Ind., Prohibits Instrumentalists from Naming Organization in Which They Play.")

All arts organizations depend on a great deal of good will in order to be successful. Right now, managements in several places are becoming masters at creating bad will in their communities.

Despite this, other orchestras have recently settled contracts peacefully. The New York Philharmonic has announced it has raised more than $90 million, even though their goal was only $50 million. The Atlanta Symphony has received a major bequest. In Honolulu, a group of citizens has emerged to attempt to bring their orchestra back to the stage, possibly with the assistance of ICSOM's great friend JoAnn Falletta.

With many orchestras succeeding, why are we not studying those places to raise the bar instead of studying our industry's managerial pot holes to lower the aspirations of entire communities? What other business emulates its failures to create a new business model?

It is the epoch of belief, it is the epoch of incredulity.

A friend of mine at one of our local universities wrote to me recently, reflecting on a lecture she had just heard and putting it in context of the news reports she has been following from Detroit. She wrote:

> *This week in graduate seminar a professor from UNC came over to tell us how he is co-opting Moore's law to design vaccines through imprint lithography. I had to look up Moore's law on Wikipedia. Here is the condensed version: In 1965, Intel co-founder Gordon Moore observed that "the number of components in integrated circuits had doubled every year from the invention of the integrated circuit in 1958 until 1965 and predicted that the trend would continue "for at least ten years""*
>
> *What is interesting to me about this is the following:*
>
> *"Although Moore's law was initially made in the form of an observation and forecast, the more widely it became accepted, the more it served as a goal for an entire industry. This drove both marketing and engineering departments of semiconductor manufacturers to focus enormous energy aiming for the specified increase in processing power that it was presumed one or*

more of their competitors would soon actually attain. In this regard, it can be viewed as a self-fulfilling prophecy.

Maybe you could come up with a kind of Moore's law for your industry based on observations of what is working and has improved over the last twenty years. Give people something to work for instead of something to work against.

All of this struck me as especially relevant. Indeed the managements who seek to create the new model by proclaiming a new apocalypticism are creating negative self-fulfilling prophecies. We must articulate positively how the field can change in order to achieve growth, to serve in even better ways, to increase relevance.

In a world that occasionally slumps with its burdens, our music is needed more than ever. We have never been more relevant.

It is the season of darkness, it is the season of light

We must not become despondent over the assault of nonsense. We must be inspired to change. Instead of "Moore's Law" we should create "ICSOM's Law", where success is expected and failure is not rewarded. Success breeds success, and failure breeds failure. Americans want to hear a positive message of advocacy, and they want to hear a message of hope. Conveniently, we have one.

Musicians everywhere must be proud and even amazed that the response to ICSOM's Call to Action to assist the musicians of the Detroit Symphony has reached $300,000, meaning that since 2007 ICSOM has raised well over $600,000 to assist our members in need. But we must do more.

In today's modern culture, the truth belongs to the people who say it most effectively. And sadly, to articulate the truth effectively you must have the funds to pursue a strategic public relations campaign. Recently a group of 400 Rabbis bought a full page ad in the *New York Times* expressing some concerns. They didn't just buy an ad—they bought news coverage and attention for their cause. But the ad itself cost $150,000.

Throughout this essay, I have enjoyed paraphrasing from Michael Steele's other favorite book, *A Tale of Two Cities*. I think how we move forward is up to us, as no one else is going to do this for us. When things are hardest is when we must be at our best. When we are surrounded by doubt we must surround ourselves with friendships and hope. The more difficult things become, the harder we must work.

Across the world, people are rising up. The musicians of ICSOM must join that movement and positively articulate our message in a way that it can be heard.

It is the best of times, it is the worst of times. It is the winter of despair, it is the spring of hope.

Supporting the Arts
Empowers the Future

INTERNATIONAL MUSICIAN
APRIL, 2011

While hiding in Holland in 1944, Anne Frank wrote in her diary "Why should millions be spent daily on the war and yet there's not a penny available for medical services, artists, or for poor people?"

Musicians from forty nations recently traveled to Amsterdam for the second International Orchestra Conference held by the International Federation of Musicians (FIM). In my opening comments there, I said "...in a world that occasionally slumps with the weight of its burdens, the musicians that comprise countless orchestras around the world offer a message of hope that citizens of every nation are eager to hear. Supporting the arts is not just a mission that keeps the past alive, but it is in fact a mission that empowers the future."

I was honored to be part of the AFM delegation and to represent ICSOM at this important gathering where musicians across the world became closer as we advocate not only for the arts but for the human spirit.

In preparing for my visit to Amsterdam, I sought out one of the most inspiring spirits the world has known, Anne Frank. I read her diary again to prepare for the experience of visiting the house where she hid for two years, but nothing quite prepares you for such emotions.

At the conference I was surrounded by musicians who have spent their lives elevating the human spirit. It was a humbling convocation of visionary thinkers and artists, and we heard the same concerns from our friends around the world that we are hearing at home.

Drastic cuts are being imposed upon the arts by vain politicians making disingenuous attempts to promote the notion that they are addressing the economic crisis by attacking fractional areas of their massive budget deficits, while continuing to fund destructive ideals and policies. This is not just an attack upon the arts, but part of an assault on workers everywhere.

One speaker stated that governments fear music because it is something they cannot control. Initially I thought that to be extreme, but then I reflected on great artists like Dmitri Shostakovich and his battle with tyranny, and the concentration camp deaths of composers such as Ervin Shulhoff. The empowering spirit of music and the role it has always played in the battle for freedom was apparent as I listened to speakers in many languages articulating the same aspirational ideals.

While listening to Brahms at Amsterdam's Concertgebouw, I saw "Liszt" carved in the balcony that surrounds the hall, along with names of other great composers. I was reminded that Anne Frank also wrote of Liszt, saying "His art was everything to him... (he) loved religious liberty and world freedom."

I realized this effort we are making is about something far greater than ourselves. Musicians approached me from Germany, France, Britain—all asking about Detroit, aware of the greatness of that orchestra and eager to hear news of the efforts to save the institution. Those same musicians were also aware of the battle for workers' rights taking place in the statehouse of Wisconsin, and in turn I became aware of struggles in The Netherlands, Argentina, Bulgaria and Brazil.

Five days later, I found myself in another of the world's greatest concert halls, Disney Hall, listening to the Los Angeles Philharmonic. The LA Phil is a thriving institution, spreading a positive message of hope and demonstrating that success can be built even in this difficult time, while music director Gustavo Dudamel proclaims: "music is a fundamental human right."

My travels for ICSOM have convinced me that while many see the landscape before us as treacherous, artists with vision can see things that others do not. Together we can imagine and create a future where our music is even more relevant to a world that endlessly seeks inspiration.

Guest Editorial, *Prelude*

BOSTON MUSICIANS' ASSOCIATION
SUMMER, 2011

Winston Churchill once said "A lie gets halfway around the world before the truth has a chance to get its pants on."

In local television news, there is an ugly phrase that often defines the tone of a newscast. "If it bleeds, it leads." Meaning, of course, that the more sensationalistic and negative a story can be, the more likely it will be the feature of the evening's newscast. This is the ideology that often finds us "teased" by promotional trailers such as "Your house is killing you...update at 6:00" or "The deadly prescription drugs in every American home...we'll tell you what you need to know."

Of course, they almost never tell us anything we really need to know, though the weather forecast is nice sometimes.

I'm afraid that the media often likes to tell the negative story, occasionally to the exclusion of the facts, especially when it is spin that is promulgated by the corporations that own the media itself. And of course, it is often true that some of the board members of our local newspapers are also on the boards for our local arts organizations, and often anti-union. This has led us to an era where the media is labeling the American orchestra an "endangered species."

I must emphasize though that this isn't true everywhere. There are many places where successful boards and successful media are promoting their communities and the arts. And I suppose that is largely the point I am trying to make.

In America, a recovery is underway, but it is felt more prominently on Wall Street than on Main Street. Even so, many arts organizations have weathered the financial storm quite well. Guidestar reports that the number of non-profits reporting a decline in contributions is decreasing, and many orchestras are promoting successes. The Colorado Symphony just reported record ticket sales for this season, and the Metropolitan Opera appears in over forty-five countries through their theater broadcasts. The Los Angeles Philharmonic and the San Francisco Symphony have become two of the most exciting non-profit arts organizations in the world while thriving in a state where the economy took a tremendous toll. And out of the ashes of the recession, the Honolulu Symphony is being promoted by a group of citizens and arts leaders determined to bring that historic orchestra back to life.

In the Commonwealth of Massachusetts alone, the Boston Symphony accounts for over $166 million dollars in economic activity every year. Across America, the arts employ over 5.7 million people, and every dollar that government invests in the arts returns seven dollars to the community.

So, why aren't these facts more prominently reported? Perhaps they don't fit a negative prejudice towards the future of the arts that exists in the media.

At this moment, newspapers are focusing on a handful of situations where unrelated circumstances have led to bankruptcy filings for several American orchestras. They try to paint this news as the end of orchestras in America as they search for ways to make each circumstance the same. It seems that the press is pretty well dominated by corporations seemingly out of touch with the communities they try to service. They are marketing a shrinking product while surrendering the role of advocate for their readers.

This negativity did not begin with the media, though. The media merely reflects what those with power project. And for years our field has been undermined by weak managers and anti-union boards that have sought to spread a message that the arts are not sustainable, and that a "new model" must be invented, all without asking if the existing model was being well implemented. And of course, "a new model" is really just a code for the anti-union thinking that seeks to undermine what the American worker has built over the last century.

It always amazes me that board members, many of whom are successful business people who would never tolerate failure in any division of the businesses they run, are so quick to accept a prediction of failure from the arts managers they hire to protect a community asset of which they are stewards. Again, I must emphasize that the vast majority of our board members are fine people who have achieved great success and who genuinely want to support the arts and their community. But how can they hear the truth over a din of negativity often supplied by their own arts managers?

Success breeds success, and failure breeds failure. There has emerged a new type of pundit for the arts in America, people writing almost glee-fully that the arts are dying. Often these words are articulated by musicians and writers whose names we otherwise would never had heard had they not managed to carve out a spotlight for themselves as the purveyors of doom. I'm afraid that they have merely established a self-fulfilling prophecy that has spread to our managements, to our boards, and to our media. We have heard these negative words before. After all, in 1970 United Press International published an article that headlined "25 Orchestras Doomed to Die" and in 1969, *Time Magazine* wrote that in the decade of the 70's we would lose as many as half of our orchestras to an economic demise. How long must we fight against this false negative rhetoric which is unsupportable by either fact or history?

It doesn't have to be this way. At this time across the world we are see-ing a rebirth of activism. In Madison, Wisconsin, as well as in courthouse squares across the country, the American worker is once again fighting for the rights of their families. Union jobs were once seen as a way for Americans to march into the middle class, allowing them to rear their families and send their children to school...to reach for the American dream and the pursuit of happiness that is guaranteed to all of us in the Declaration of Independence. But now these very jobs are under attack, using the economic downturn as a decoy while pursuing a different agenda. And we are seeing the results, both in an erosion of the middle class and a lack of community investment from the wealthiest among us.

The disparity of wealth in America has never been greater than it is today. There is more wealth, and more poverty, in America than anyone could have dreamt even thirty years ago. In the 1970's, the wealthiest 1% of Americans took in about 9% of the income. Today, that same 1% takes in over 23% of the nation's income.

Yet there are politicians that would have you believe that workers are earning too much. And there are community leaders that would have you believe that the citizens of our cities and their children cannot have what they deserve when it comes to the arts and education.

As politicians propose cut after cut for our children, they also propose no cuts for our nation's most fortunate, the 1% that absorbs so much of the nation's income. The value of arts education cannot be disputed. Study after study has demonstrated that children who are exposed to music are far more likely to stay in school, participate in after school activities, and enjoy learning. This has been known and accepted as far back as Aristotle, who wrote in his treatise *Politics* that "Enough has been said to show that music has a power of forming the character, and should therefore be introduced into the education of the young."

So, what can we do? Well, first we must not panic, as panic is the enemy of reason. We must instead increase our unity while educating ourselves with a message of positive advocacy for our orchestras, our communities, our children, and for live music of all styles. We must not allow someone else's negativity, propaganda and agenda to become our self-fulfilling prophecy. We must say this clearly, positively, and in a media-astute way...there is no crisis for the arts in America. The crisis lies in arts management.

If we can positively articulate our vision of a future where our communities can achieve what they deserve, then there can be no doubt that our musicians can continue to be investments that bring cultural, educational, and economic returns for the communities where our children learn and our companies do business.

When Winston Churchill made his statement about how quickly a lie can get around the world, he was dealing with the media as it existed in 1940. Today, the internet provides unedited platforms for almost every idea, positive or negative, true or false. It is, unfortunately, the side effect of an anonymous and instantaneous method of communication that gives us the ability to communicate instantly without saying anything at all. In 1992, Bob Dylan wrote "Technology to wipe out the truth is now available. Not everybody can afford it but it's available. When the cost comes down, look out!" Well, in 2010, the cost has clearly come down.

As musicians and American laborers, we must educate our

communities, our audiences, our boards, our friends, and even those who stand against us about the value of what we do. We must positively articulate a deeper truth as we seek to serve our communities, even if that truth might not end up leading the evening news.

Leonard Leibowitz,
December 15, 1938- October 3, 2011

SENZA SORDINO
NOVEMBER, 2011

When the complete archive of *Senza Sordino* was posted on the ICSOM website, I spent hours reading through issue after issue. It is clear just from that source that no person had a greater influence over the gains of orchestral musicians during the past fifty years than Leonard Leibowitz.

I found a 1974 entry from my own orchestra, long before I joined, which said "We feel the sense of solidarity and pride we have discovered is a direct result of the inspiration of Len Leibowitz." I'm certain that at one point or another, every orchestra in the country might have been able to make such a statement. Perhaps no single person has ever been a more dedicated influence or a stronger advocate for musicians in the field of symphonic music in America.

He was brilliant, inspiring, legendary, charismatic, witty...and frustrating.

Lenny was a New Yorker through and through. He never re-set his watch from New York time, no matter where he was in the world. I was never with him even one day when he did not complete the *New York Times* crossword puzzle, always in ink.

He had one of the fastest minds I have ever known, and one of the quickest wits. One time I failed to understand a legal concept he was trying to explain to me, and in apologizing for my follow-up questions I began with "Please indulge my ignorance, but..." and before the sound of my words could taper he interrupted with "Bruce I have been indulging your ignorance since I met you."

He was a legend. It was exciting to be by his side. When he teased you, he made you feel part of an exclusive club. When he complimented you, he made you feel brilliant. He could write amazingly quickly. At one ICSOM conference, we asked for a last minute resolution calling for AFM Unity during a time of difficulties between two other groups in the union. Within two minutes he had produced a full resolution on yellow legal paper, beautifully worded, and written in pen without a single crossed out word, like a Mozart score. I went back afterwards to find the torn paper, and I have it right beside me as I am writing this.

During his tenure with ICSOM, he was known simply as "DILC"— Distinguished ICSOM Legal Counsel.

Everyone has their favorite Lenny story. Mine might be the time when we were in New York, on 48th Street around midnight in an April chill. I was staying at a hotel there, and he was trying to get a ride up to 86th Street. It was raining, and the black cars-for-hire were circulating after the Theater crowd had dissipated.

One car pulled up and Lenny said "86th Street, how much?"

The driver answered "Fifteen dollars."

Lenny said "Ten bucks." And the driver just moved on. The scene then repeated itself numerous times.

We stood there in the rain for twenty minutes until Lenny got one of those cars to take him home for ten bucks.

For someone who was so constantly generous with his time and himself, he could also be very private. For several years I urged him to write a book about his life, and even tried to help him get started. I told him that he would end up liking the book a lot better if he wrote it than if I did. But he was at times hesitant to review his personal history.

Eventually we got close enough that he would tell me some things about his life. He had a brother who was an artist that died young, and his father had been a photojournalist for the *New York Times*. His father covered the sports beat and the Yankees, which is where Lenny's life-long love for the pinstripes began. As a kid he would go to work with his father, and occasionally hang out in the dugout at Yankee Stadium, meeting some of the greatest players in baseball history. His knowledge of baseball was encyclopedic, and in some ways the best place to talk with him was at a baseball game. The last game I saw with him was the Texas Rangers vs. the Minnesota Twins, in August of 2007, and I still have both our tickets stubs (tickets he was somehow able to make me buy of course!)

One night we were going to meet at a restaurant in San Francisco, but he was a little late. He came down and said he had been watching ESPN Classic on the hotel cable system, and they were showing a boxing match from the Fifties. In the old film, he saw his father at ringside taking pictures, and he just couldn't stop watching.

It seems poignant that I find myself writing this on a night when the Yankees were knocked out of the playoffs for this year.

In 2005 I wrote an article about Lenny and a 5:00 am e-mail exchange between the two of us. We were debating economics and the arts, and Lenny wrote one of the most profound appeals for beauty I may have ever read, certainly from a lawyer and not a poet. He wrote:

> *"I wish that there would be no need for the artist to justify governmental and corporate support of great music by arguing its value in financial terms as if it were a commodity, like pig futures, or any other kind of 'business'. Wouldn't the artists be better equipped to demonstrate the intrinsic values of refreshment of the human spirit, the recognition of beauty, and the contribution to nurturing and raising truly civilized and cultured men and women that are the real assets of art? Shouldn't it be the business leaders, e.g., our own Board members, and other interested individuals, corporate and governmental figures, who report on the economic impact of the arts to their business? After all, they are supposed to be the experts, indeed, the 'trustees' of the financial health of the community. As the old business slogan goes, 'If it's good for General Motors, it's good for America'. If that is true, ought it not to be those running 'General Motors' to tell us what impact music and other visual and performing arts have made, and continue to make, to the fiscal common good? But instead, in today's North American Society, it has become the artists themselves who*

must be the sales personnel of their art form in the context of its economic value rather than the intrinsic value of their passion, their talent, and their ability to take the rest of us down the paths to some of life's finest moments."

There is not one musician working in an American orchestra today, of any generation, who doesn't owe a part of his or her livelihood to the work of Lenny Leibowitz. Lenny was ICSOM Counsel until 2010, but the benefits won for musicians by Lenny's tireless efforts and commitment to the art of music continue. That will remain true for years to come.

Of course, there were difficulties too. No man is perfect, and larger than life figures come with flaws. It doesn't benefit the memory of any man to portray him as a saint. But in my mind and my heart, I remember Lenny tonight at his very best—and his best was more than we had the right to ask of anyone.

Goodbye Lenny. Thank you for everything. I wish I could have seen you just once more.

Perspective: The Power
of Positive Action

SYMPHONY MAGAZINE
WINTER, 2012

How to create a strong future for orchestras? Those invested in our industry must not yield to pessimism.

In my travels as Chairman of the International Conference of Symphony and Opera Musicians (ICSOM), I have visited with many of America's orchestras, from San Juan to Honolulu. This journey has afforded me a unique view of symphony orchestras, as I try to meet with as wide a segment of each orchestra's constituency as possible. I am backstage with the musicians in their lounges, and also in their homes. I meet with the board leaders, CEOs, and occasionally members of the staff. I ask the musicians to take me to meet their audiences and supporters, all the while listening for the reasons for success, and also the causes of failure.

Unfortunately, all too often I find a negative perception of the future of orchestras, presented as an assumption of inevitability. But when I ask why such a perception exists, many are hard pressed to articulate reasons that haven't been supplied for them by negative studies, blogs, or articles.

I am left with one overwhelming realization: the way things are is not the way things have to be.

We live in a time when, for better or worse, the truth belongs to those who say it most effectively. In this media age, words have incredible power, and the words we choose in discussing our field have ramifications. At a time when musicians have made tremendous sacrifices in recognition of economic realities, too seldom do we hear the sound of our music matched by the sound of CEOs and board leaders making compelling cases for their orchestras. When the field uses negative terms to describe itself, it does not inspire the donors, audiences, and politicians we need to support us.

Some of this, I fear, is born of the culture within our field, where conflicts do exist in the labor-management relationship. These internal conflicts actually don't concern me when they remain internal. After all, everyone in this field loves art; and art is largely based on the open exploration of human emotion. It seems reasonable to me that at times people immersed in the world of art will have disagreements. But for the good of our communities and future generations of Americans, we must resist a temptation to merely want to win. We should resist using harsh language when debating those who disagree with us, and we should not undermine our highest aspirations by indulging in our basest instincts.

We must effectively market our orchestras, promoting them as vital and branding them as indispensable. In a world where other businesses that offer far less to the common good have mastered the art of promotion and the utilization of free media, many orchestras remain behind the times.

About our field, we hear "unsustainability" and equally destructive terms from people who observe us from afar, sometimes without really having a vested interest in the success or failure of our orchestras. Far too often their negative words are recited from within our field.

People will donate to, and invest in, organizations that inspire them, and they will not invest in organizations that question their own sustainability.

We must stop listening to and giving forums to extremists. The problem is not the musicians' union or the economy or the League of American Orchestras. The problem is one of national perception, and we can only change that by joining together and becoming public advocates for the arts, for our orchestras, and for the children who might never be exposed to this great music. By engaging in our current negative national public dialogue, we are merely supplying donors and political leaders with reasons to avoid supporting us.

The message regarding education should be an easy sell. The value of music in education has been observed as far back as Aristotle, who wrote,

"Enough has been said to show that music has a power of forming the character, and should therefore be introduced into the education of the young." Before him, Plato went even further by saying, "I would teach the children music, physics, and philosophy, but the most important is music, for in the patterns of the arts are the keys to all learning."

Wouldn't it benefit every orchestra, every musician, every manager, and every board member if we were more prepared to recite these phrases rather than "structural deficit" or financial analysis from Stanford?

I frequently receive calls from musicians asking for advocacy information requested by a particular board member. The trustee tells the musicians how often their board meetings take a negative direction, discussing only what *cannot* be achieved instead of what *is* possible. The trustee wants to speak up but feels intimidated. So I supply them with facts they can spread to their friends and community contacts—facts that stand in contrast to the messages often read in their newspapers.

Key to these advocacy points is the effect of the arts in the local community. I deeply believe that the solution for success in any orchestra lies in its ability to reflect its own community. In that regard, many of our national conversations don't provide much local insight. In fact, many of those conversations use terms that often undermine an orchestra's ability to brand itself within its own city. In that regard, no two constituencies of an orchestra are better equipped to work towards the same positive goal of community branding than the musicians and the board. They are the ones who have lived longest within the community, and they are the ones who have invested the most time in attending the schools, meeting the residents, and electing the political leaders of their town. Managers and music directors tend to change locations more frequently than musicians and board members, and they should seek the input of the two groups that know the community better than most. Managers should foster a relationship between those two groups, as they would best be able to direct the manager's skills toward uniquely serving the community.

Sadly, in too many places I have visited, I see walls built between the board and the musicians instead of bridges. The destructive rhetoric that permeates our national discussion further widens the chasm.

A Rhetoric of Negativity

I often think that those who advocate major change for our field are simply going about it all wrong. How can we fail to see that destructive rhetoric is the enemy of change?

Our field appears to be emulating the sociopolitical environment of Washington. We aren't talking to each other; we are not listening to each other. We are staking out positions that paint us into stereotypical corners.

No business, and no society really, can make a case that its workers are earning too much while those same workers see others making quite sizeable increases within the same field. Musicians are willing to sacrifice precisely because they *do* love their orchestras and they *do* love their communities. Labeling the salaries of musicians as out of control at the moment of their greatest sacrifice breeds resentment, and resentment thwarts debate. It simply does not promote positive dialogue, and only serves to make the musicians resistant to change.

There is no doubt that our field faces challenges. But why would we promote those challenges more vociferously than we promote our own orchestras? No other field does this to itself. Look at the food industry—according to American Express, 90 percent of restaurants fail in their first year of business, but no one within the restaurant industry would publicly suggest that Americans no longer like to eat!

When the United States ended the Space Shuttle program recently, I thought back 50 years to one of the greatest American speeches ever delivered. On May 25, 1961, John F. Kennedy challenged America to land a man on the moon and return him safely to earth by the end of the decade. On that day he said, "While we cannot guarantee that we shall one day be first, we can guarantee that any failure on our part to make these efforts shall make us last." In that speech he said that Americans strive to achieve great things not because they are easy, but because they are hard. He told an Irish folk tale where two young boys on a journey confront a stone wall, too high to mount but too long to circumvent. Facing the prospect of a retreat that would end their adventure, one boy threw the hat of the other over the wall, leaving them no choice but to find some way to overcome the obstacle. Kennedy spoke in a time when America dreamt of what could be achieved, what could be built, and what could be created.

We must engage in positive advocacy and education of the public. A recent poll indicated that 40 percent of Americans believe that as much as 5 percent of the federal budget goes to support the arts. A shocking 7 percent of respondents said they thought the government spent *half* of its budget on arts programs. This is the misconception we deal with in a world of spin where the truth is often a victim of sound bites. In reality, the entire amount of the federal budget spent on the National Endowment for the Arts, the National Endowment for the Humanities, and the Corporation for Public Broadcasting is only .066%. And every dollar that the government invests in this way returns seven dollars to the community.

Celebrating Success

I believe that we can still achieve a great future, but to get there we must change our rhetoric. We must stop supplying reporters with ready-made destructive copy. We must not give our communities reasons to avoid supporting us.

Specifically, I would urge a moratorium on the phrase "The New Model." For a phrase that has absolutely no meaning, it is powerfully destructive to relationships everywhere.

Other fields, with far less to offer, have mastered the art of messaging. The "truth" they sell is in their message; but even if you have an effective truth, it will not be heard unless you also have an effective message. On a national basis, our field does not have such a message. It does not serve anyone in our field to suggest that student musicians would be an adequate replacement for one of the world's greatest orchestras, or to call musicians "stubborn" in the press because they needed several days to consider accepting a massive pay cut.

Thankfully, many orchestras do have an effective message locally. In those places we see orchestras increasing their relevance in inspiring ways. And in places where orchestras are failing, the reasons for those failures are uniquely local as well.

The prevailing view of orchestras is that they have suffered in the recession, but I don't see it that way. To me, the point to be made is how wonderful and remarkable it is that many of our orchestras have done well in this climate. That is the story we should work together to promote. We cannot afford to allow ourselves to see only the darkness without acknowledging the light. I urge us not to promote failure while ignoring success.

I see those success stories as inspirational and reassuring for a future I know we can achieve. As Molière wrote, "The best way to predict the future is to create it." The quality of American orchestras has never been greater, and I see a future where orchestras are even more relevant, where we reach a wider audience, and where more and more young people are eager to be a part of something that represents quality at a time when the world accepts mediocrity. We have resources in our organizations that other businesses ache for. We have musicians who inspire, we have board members who want to serve their cities, we have managers who want to ensure that our orchestras thrive, and we have audiences that love us.

I have never been more optimistic or inspired about what we can do. That is the truth we should be articulating, and that is the alert we should be sounding. Until then, I want everyone to take a deep breath. I don't want to hear one more negative word, read one more erroneous report, or find even one more orchestra silenced. We must not be afraid to dream great dreams simply because they are hard to achieve. While we cannot guarantee success, we can guarantee failure if we continue to engage in negative public rhetoric. We owe better to Beethoven, to Bernstein, to our teachers, to our students, to our children, to our audiences…and to ourselves.

The way things are is not the way things have to be.

The Autumn of Our Discontent: Orchestral Musicians and the Crisis in Arts Management

OCTOBER 12, 2012
WWW.ICSOM.ORG

On September 24 in Seattle, inexperienced replacement workers finally seemed to capture America's attention. With the referees of the National Football League locked out by a League of billionaire owners, a series of nationally televised blunders came to a head when the replacement officials essentially handed a victory to the Seattle Seahawks over the Green Bay Packers in what many observers consider a blown call of epic proportions.

Twitter was flooded with outrage. The NFL players cursed the un-skilled, non-union officials, and even anti-union political figures expressed their outrage at the situation, in effect supporting the locked-out referees of the NFL Referee Association. With such pressure in support of the excellence of the locked-out officials, it came as no surprise that within 48 hours a deal to end the lockout was reached, with the referees holding on to their pension for the term of the agreement.

If Americans are outraged to see inexperienced, non-union workers damage their spectator sporting events, you think they might care more about how the future of the country would be affected by having an unskilled, non-union labor force teaching our children or serving our communities through public and private sector jobs.

It is wonderful that politicians are Green Bay Packers fans, but one can only imagine the influence they could have for American families if they were also greater fans of teachers, public and private workers, artists, and musicians.

Lockouts and Silence

For the American worker, it is the autumn of our discontent. The musicians of America's symphony orchestras are facing the same difficulties of other workers in a climate that mirrors the greater socio-economic environment of the country. America's orchestras are non-profit organizations, but just as in the for-profit world, executive compensation rises as worker pay decreases.

Managements of symphony orchestras are also following the pattern of the for-profit world, becoming more aggressive in negotiations and resorting more frequently to lockouts. Just this fall, the musicians of the Atlanta Symphony, the Indianapolis Symphony, and the Minnesota Orchestra have been locked out by their managements, and their communities have been deprived of music. Lockouts potentially await even more orchestras. As the *New York Times* reported this year "America's unionized workers, buffeted by layoffs and stagnating wages, face another phenomenon that is increasingly throwing them on the defensive: lockouts."

We live in a time when labor is under attack. As Robert Reich has written, the median male worker earns less today (when adjusted for inflation) than 30 years ago, and as a result the working class that made America great struggles. In the 1970's, the wealthiest 1% of Americans took in about 9% of the nation's income. Today, that same 1% absorbs over 23% of the nation's income.

The economics for symphony orchestras are even more complex, as orchestras depend on the philanthropic nature of America's citizens, and as wealth becomes more centralized, organizations need to have a message that inspires those with wealth to donate to, and invest in, artistic institutions. The reasons to be articulated for the continued support of our orchestras are compelling.

The Arts and the Economy

Purely from an economic standpoint, the arts are good business. According to Americans for the Arts, the non-profit arts and culture industry accounts for over $135 billion in economic activity every year, and leads to over 4 million full-time jobs for Americans. In many of our cities, symphony orchestras (along with opera and ballet) are the most prominent performing arts organization, and the most visible ambassadors for the community.

City governments and business leaders are quick to invest in performing arts centers, recognizing that when symphony concerts take place, business occurs downtown. Restaurants have waiting lists, cab drivers work, parking lots are full, and post-concert cafes and bars are filled with arts attendees. Everyone benefits, even if they might never attend a concert themselves.

But it makes no sense to invest in buildings without preserving the institutions that live there. In Minneapolis, the management of the Minnesota Orchestra is proposing a $40,000 pay cut per musician even as they spend over $50 million in renovating the lobby of their concert hall.

The impact of music on education has never been disputed, even by those who have no desire to fund such programs. The musicians of America's orchestras spend countless hours each day with the next generation of Americans, giving them tools that multiple studies demonstrate will enhance their cognitive ability and even their health well into their seventies.

While the recession has had an impact on all Americans, and certainly on philanthropic giving, the story to be told is not that some orchestras have suffered, but rather that so many have done so well. Numerous orchestras are seeing increases in donations, ticket sales, and attendance. An article about the St. Louis Symphony recently proclaimed that it had just experienced its best year in a decade.

The Resiliency of Orchestras

In fact, arts giving is recovering from the depths of the recession at twice the rate of other charitable giving, and according to Giving USA, arts giving in America increased last year by 4.1%, to a total of $13.12 billion. The presence of orchestras in our communities is financially beneficial. A recent report demonstrated that the Buffalo Philharmonic has an economic impact of $25 million annually in the city of Buffalo, while a 2008 study showed that the Boston Symphony alone has an impact of $166 million in the Commonwealth of Massachusetts.

But these are not the facts being told in the press, where the media seeks to portray a handful of orchestra bankruptcies as evidence of spreading failure for the art form. It just isn't true. Many of the challenges to the progress made by America's orchestral musicians are born of ideology and not economy.

The fact is that there is no crisis in classical music...the crisis is in arts management.

Non-profit symphony orchestras are governed by boards, most of whom are wonderful people who truly love music, their orchestras, and their communities. But, most of them now come from the for-profit world, and they hire "industry professionals" to manage their non-profit organizations. The board members tend to take their education for running a non-profit from the "industry professionals."

If that industry professional can present evidence that orchestras everywhere are failing, then they can increase their salary simply by somehow managing to keep the doors open, which usually means reducing the cost of the work force and eliminating concerts, which in turn reduces revenue generating opportunities.

This is a short sighted approach of course, as orchestras depend on the ability to attract and retain the finest musicians in order to fulfill their mission; a mission which, by the way, is not measured in financial terms.

Non-profits arts organizations and orchestras do not exist to balance their budgets; they exist to serve the community for the greater good. They should seek to be fiscally responsible as a way of achieving their mission, which is always community service and the performance of great music at the highest level. While financial stability is needed, it is not the measure of success for a non-profit arts institution. And clearly, locking out musicians does not serve the mission of a performing arts organization.

The "New" Apocalypticism

The tendency of orchestra managers to present a negative view of the future is not unprecedented, but it is bewildering, and it is a poor fund raising message. People will donate to organizations that inspire them and that serve their communities, but they will not invest in organizations that question their own sustainability.

The good news to be told about the orchestral field's negativity is that all of this destructiveness is nothing new, and the proponents of this negativity are no more accurate today than they were decades ago. As mind-boggling as it seems, the field seems to have been dedicated to promoting its own demise for quite some time now. Every few years a new report comes out that suggests that orchestras are not sustainable and that a new model must be discovered. It is always called something slightly different, such as "The New Paradigm" or "The New Economic Reality", or simply "The New Model" but it is always the same. I've taken to calling it "The New Apocalypticism."

We can trace this phenomenon back quite a long way.

An article from United Press International was titled *25 Orchestras Doomed to Die*, and it forecast the demise of 25 symphony orchestras throughout America. This would be terrible news, except this article was published in 1970, and the predictions have been proven wrong for forty years.

It went on to say (remember, in 1970) that "orchestras have one alternative to going out of business." They must "reshape—either by reducing the size of orchestras from 100 to 90 musicians or by shortening seasons."

Does any of this sound familiar?

An article from June of 1969, published in *Time Magazine*, quoted "an expert in orchestral finances" as saying "Between 1971 and 1973, we stand a very good chance of losing at least one-third, if not half of our major symphony orchestras."

Time has proven *Time Magazine* wrong.

We have a document from the president of the board of the Chicago Symphony, who wrote:

"The (Chicago Symphony) now must solve a problem which has arisen from economic conditions beyond its control. A deficit has been incurred, and undoubtedly there will be annual deficits for some years to come. This affects the future of the orchestra."

And he continued:

"Our problem does not differ in kind from the financial problem that faces each of the major orchestras in the United States."

This is especially alarming, isn't it?...that an orchestra as great as the Chicago Symphony could face this predicament. I would be more concerned had this not been written on April 1, 1940.

There is one great sentence in this 1940 document though. In a message that all managers should heed, especially today, the board chair states:

"We cannot reduce our expenses below our present level without seriously endangering our standard of symphony music, which would soon result in endangering our principal source of income."

And therein lies the predicament: orchestra managers, and their board members, with the assistance of negative rhetoric provided for them by skewed and flawed studies, disproven over decades, are now once again articulating the need for a new business model, while failing to recognize a basic tenet of industry: no business ever solved a financial problem by offering an inferior product to its public.

The Birth of ICSOM

Fifty years ago, in Chicago in 1962, orchestra musicians created a revolution with the founding of the International Conference of Symphony and Opera Musicians (ICSOM).

1962 was a time of great difficulty for orchestra musicians. There was almost no job security, and annual income hovered around $5000. Symphonic players were treated terribly, and the dean of the Indiana University School of Music, Wilfred Bain, said "people who push brooms are treated better than symphony players." Musicians were excluded from participating in the ratification of their contracts, and benefits such as health care and pensions were non-existent.

The past 50 years since the creation of ICSOM, it could be argued, have been a golden age for classical music in America. With the ability of musicians to earn a living, care for their families, and truly put down roots in their communities, America's orchestras of all budgets sizes have become recognized as the very best in the world. The musicians of our orchestras have elevated their communities, taught countless children, and enhanced the business environment for their towns.

Through the short sighted attempts at diminishing the workplaces for musicians that our managements are currently aggressively pursuing, all of that is at risk now.

The Demonization of the American Worker

There was a time when the demonization of the American worker was a losing proposition for any political or public leader. After all, the Norris-LaGuardia Act of 1932 proclaimed "the individual unorganized worker is genuinely helpless to exercise actually liberty…"

It seems wistfully poetic now to see the words "liberty" and "worker" stated as part of an American law. Companies once considered well-treated employees as conducive to a productive work force. But now, too often companies see workers as replaceable parts.

Even though the artists of America's orchestras are considered among the best in the world, it appears as if boards and managements view musicians as entirely replaceable as well, in a phenomenon that Chicago area attorney Kevin Case recently referred to as "the commoditization of symphony orchestra musicians."

Solidarity and Hope

There is always good news to be found, and musicians will continue to serve their communities and future generations. While union member-ship has decreased in our country, that isn't true for orchestral performers. The musicians of ICSOM perform for our audiences in a spirit of solidarity and support for each other through a united network of friends. Orchestral musicians are overwhelmingly members of the American Federation of Musicians, even in Right-to-Work states. Classical music is everywhere, and attendance for our concerts is rebounding from the depths of the recession. Indeed, it is a testament to the viability of America's orchestras that so many have withstood the barrage of negativity unleashed upon us by our managements.

In this climate of unnecessarily aggressive negotiating tactics, anti-union leaders use "kids first, unions last" as a slogan. How can they not realize that by putting unions last they are inevitably putting their children, and their nation, last as well?

There is much more than a touchdown at stake. Currently at stake is the question of what kind of country we want to be, and what kind of children we want to rear. American orchestras have grown to be considered among the very best in the world, and once that is lost our cities will never be able to develop such valuable assets again.

When the United States ended the Space Shuttle program recently, I couldn't help but think back fifty years to one of the greatest American speeches ever delivered. On May 25, 1961, John F. Kennedy challenged America to land a man on the moon and return him safely to earth by the end of the decade. On that day he said "While we cannot guarantee that we shall one day be first, we can guarantee that any failure on our part to make these efforts shall make us last." In that speech he said that Americans strive to achieve great things not because they are easy, but because they are hard. He told an Irish folk tale where two young boys on a journey confront a stone wall, too high to mount but too long to circumvent. Facing the prospect of a retreat that would end their adventure, one boy threw the hat of the other over the wall, leaving them no choice to but find some way to overcome this obstacle.

Kennedy spoke in a time when America dreamt of what could be achieved, what could be built, and what could be created. He spoke without any assumption that there was anything that we could not achieve for our children.

At a time that could appear bleak for all American workers, we must see every crisis as an opportunity. Those who seek to undermine the rights of teachers, policemen, firefighters, and musicians will find a stronger, more dedicated and more unified spirit among us And for the musical artists of America, at a time when there are many who doubt America's orchestras, we will not doubt ourselves.

Bloggin' (on a Sunday afternoon)

SENZA SORDINO
NOVEMBER, 2012

I really should know better by now. I should know not to read the comments section on any article anywhere, whether it is about a sporting event or a political campaign or (perhaps especially) an orchestra. Far too often these comments provide an unedited forum for hatred and resentment often spewed by isolated people who find themselves irresistibly offered a vast internet of readers they believe might actually care about their unenlightened and hopeless observations.

I have learned to avoid those types of comments, or at least overlook them, as I shake my head and move on unaffected. Surprisingly though, the comment sections to a few recent articles on orchestras have actually provided for some legitimate observations and debate, but I'm afraid I have at times found those observations just as disheartening.

In this time of difficulty for orchestras, there is a legitimate debate about the future that needs to be held, and it needs to be held in a responsible manner. Writers of blogs should be especially careful in presenting their facts, if not their opinions. And those who react should do so with as much information as possible, or the debate will only be stifled.

When the president of a major music conservatory writes a blog on the *Huffington Post* stating that the San Antonio Symphony has been on strike or locked out this season, it does harm to the entire debate. As we all know, the musicians of the San Antonio Symphony have reached a settlement after a difficult negotiation, without a work stoppage, and are now looking to advance their orchestra as they move into a new concert hall in their upcoming 75th anniversary season.

I have personally never commented on an article on a news website, or on a blog. It seems to me that occasionally words can come too easily when responding. Sometime you might read an article that angers you, or frustrates you, and you've hit "send" before you've really thought it through. While I hold the position of ICSOM Chair, I feel an obligation to choose my words carefully and to seek the input of our incredibly thoughtful Governing Board and our legal counsel before releasing my statements.

But I do discover now and then that I make intermittent appearances in the comments sections. I find reassurance, though, in knowing that most of what it is represented does not reflect anything I have actually said.

Recently I was reading the comments to an article that I did not write, though a piece I did write was referenced in the article. Several comments were made by someone who is apparently a staff member for an orchestra somewhere, and I have to admit that the comments were hurtful, because they did not reflect views ever expressed by ICSOM.

I've been through this before, and more personally. Last year, after my keynote address at the University of Michigan, a blogger accused me of "doing a disservice to his (ICSOM's) membership" even though his criticism didn't accurately reflect anything I actually said. The attack was easy for me to dismiss though, as it is hard to know how seriously I am supposed to take someone who uses a picture of a talking cat to accuse me of not being serious.

But the recent comments from the staffer really did disturb me. The commenter wrote:

> These are heady times for the International Conference of Symphony Orchestra (sic)Musicians (ICSOM) and their ilk. True, their tuxes and tails have grown a tad more maggot-ridden since their early labor movement days. But churning out full-throated, endowment-consuming zombie musicians has proven decidedly lucrative.

That's all fine so far. The commenter is engaging in sarcasm and parody reflective of the sarcasm in the article being addressed. While I know that musicians took some prurient pleasure in that sarcasm, ICSOM didn't write it, nor is the writer a member of ICSOM.

But the commenter goes further:

> ...*musicians would rather lumber up and down the sidewalk with picket signs than accept their share of the rational diet everyone else has had to be on for a long, long time.*

Well, here is where the commenter injures the dialogue. Truth be told, with the exception of about 36 hours, all of the recent work stoppages in ICSOM orchestras have been lockouts. Of our own will, musicians haven't chosen to carry any signs.

And then:

> *Musicians, ravenous for entitlements, never cease their demands for more and more and more. Hardly a week goes by without another screaming imbecile in a tuxedo crying "unfair!" and demanding more, and more, and more, while the hardworking staff and administrators struggle to keep food on the table for them.*

Well, "imbecile"? That is pretty unfortunate. But, I understand. The commenter seems angry.

And then, yet even more:

> *Why is it that such outrageously bad behavior toward their staff colleagues is not only tolerated in this industry, it's openly encouraged by the AFM, ICSOM and their members?*

These are tough times, and I'm sure that in hindsight the commenter would have phrased these comments differently. But, I would like to be clear about a few things, because I do share the concerns of those who worry that the dialogue is becoming so nasty that it will do irreparable damage. So, let me review what ICSOM has said.

On multiple occasions, I have urged our members not to cast aspersions. I have written in *Symphony* magazine (the publication of the League of American Orchestras) that the way things are is not the way things have to be, and that the destructive rhetoric that permeates our national discussion only widens the chasm. I have called upon the leadership of the League of American Orchestras to make similar public statements to their membership, but unfortunately as yet they have not done so.

It is true that I offered criticism of the League during my University of Michigan keynote address, but I made those statements in the presence of the League's leadership and not in anonymous late night comment sections on blogs. Even that criticism followed a face-to-face conversation a few months earlier where I urged the League to make a statement distancing itself from the negative rhetoric of one of its board members. I told the president of the League that if he did not distance himself, and his organization, the chasm between the League and musicians would inevitably widen into destructive dialogue.

I was unfortunately dismissed, and my prediction has equally unfortunately been proven true.

But universally, the musicians of ICSOM care deeply about their staff members. Many of them are in the same position we are, facing serious cutbacks while those above them gain dramatic pay increases. And the staff, not being in a union, all too often doesn't have someone who can speak in their defense. If I can do that more effectively, I assure every staff member toiling away for his or her orchestra's mission on small salaries that I will be their advocate as well.

The message we have repeatedly delivered in this time of difficulty is that if conversations need to be held, they can't be held under duress. As I wrote in my *Symphony* article, I often think that those who advocate major change for our field are simply going about it all wrong. How can we fail to see that destructive rhetoric is the enemy of change?

Sadly, at a time when we should all be pulling together, it is the musicians who find themselves targeted and demonized...even called "imbeciles." But through positive messages, the musicians facing lockouts are gaining tremendous support from their communities. The musicians offer a message of hope, music, and spiritual and economic revitalization. Sadly, certain managements and boards are offering only silence and deprivation.

The musicians of our orchestras are just like the majority of the staff members of our orchestras; we believe in our cause, and we are hurting unnecessarily.

Music Brings Solace in the Face of Tragedy

INTERNATIONAL MUSICIAN
FEBRUARY, 2013

On December 15, the locked-out Musicians of the Minnesota Orchestra produced their own concert at a moment when America was preparing to celebrate a subdued holiday season following the senseless tragedy of Sandy Hook Elementary, where twenty children and six teachers lost their lives to gun violence.

Covering the emotional event, the St. Paul *Pioneer-Press*, wrote:

> "This is why we need orchestras. Because when life confronts you with something profoundly painful, such as an elementary-school massacre, you can find sanctuary and salve in a concert hall, a forum in which a composer can reach across centuries and comfort you not with a means of escape but with a deep and powerful wisdom beyond words about what it means to be human."

I was reminded of how often our country has had to face tragedy, and how music has played an instrumental role in bringing us all together at times of national pain.

In my collection of thousands of vinyl records, perhaps the most significant is a live recording of the Boston Symphony performing Mozart's *Requiem*, recorded on January 19, 1964, in memory of John F. Kennedy, less than two months following the assassination that traumatized the nation.

As Leonard Bernstein said following President Kennedy's assassination: "This will be our reply to violence: to make music more intensely, more beautifully, more devotedly than ever before."

Thirty-seven years later, in the weeks following September 11, 2001, orchestras across the world performed as a testament that humanity will always persevere in the face of violence, and that music will forever be a response to hatred.

The November, 2001 issue of the *International Musician* stated "Music has played an indispensable role in the ongoing process of healing the nation, following the terrorist assaults on New York and Washington, DC. Coast to coast and around the world, musicians have come together to help bring solace to grieving people."

I vividly remember playing Mozart's *Requiem* that September in the Chapel of Duke University with the North Carolina Symphony in a concert that raised $30,000 to assist the families of the victims of the 9/11 attacks. That week in the *New York Times*, Bernard Holland wrote "Art is our fragile claim to control over our lives. Terrorism offered only uncertainty."

In many religions, the celebration of Christmas is followed closely by the marking of Holy Innocent's Day, or Children's Mass. This year, as I again played in the pit for numerous performances of Tchaikovsky's *Nutcracker*, I couldn't help but think of the children of Sandy Hook as I watched the young dancers on stage in the party scene, and as I looked to the audiences to see so many young people mesmerized by the dancing and the music.

I was deeply affected by the December 15 episode of *Saturday Night Live*, which featured the New York City Children's Chorus reverently singing *Silent Night* in recognition of the loss of innocence we all felt as a nation following the Sandy Hook tragedy.

The *SNL* musical guest that evening was Paul McCartney, who was joined by the Children's Chorus for his holiday hit *Wonderful Christmastime*, just as the lyrics say:

> "The choir of children sing their song. They practiced
> all year long."

Mr. McCartney was singing live from Rockefeller Center, just 22 city blocks from where his legendary songwriting partner John Lennon was also a victim of gun violence. For a certain generation of classical musicians, John Lennon's senseless death has been a part of our musical lives. He was literally shot down on Leonard Bernstein's doorstep, as they were neighbors in The Dakota on West 72nd Street.

It is music that brings us together. It is music that heals our wounds, soothes our souls, celebrates our happiness, and binds us together, not only as a nation, but as humans. In an attic in Amsterdam, Anne Frank wrote of Liszt and Beethoven. In America, following terrorist attacks, the world turned to our orchestras, and Mozart, for comfort. And again, following Sandy Hook, comfort was found in a performance of the Musicians of the Minnesota Orchestra.

There are many reasons why every community needs its orchestra. But in the review that celebrated the Musicians of the Minnesota Orchestra for bringing their community together at a time of need, an unfortunate and painful reminder of the destructiveness of the lockout those musicians currently face ended the writer's thoughts: "But sadness lurked in the knowledge that the orchestra is about to slide back into silence as the lockout lingers on."

The Myth of the Graying Audience

SENZA SORDINO
MARCH, 2013

On New Year's morning, I rolled over as my clock radio turned on to NPR's *Morning Edition*, as it does every morning far earlier than I ever expect. This day I was surprised to hear my own voice during a feature on the state of orchestras in America from a phone interview I had done some weeks earlier. The reporter introduced me as a bassist "with the South Carolina Symphony," a fact I found even more surprising than hearing my own voice. I felt fairly certain, even in my relative slumber, that I had never been a member of the South Carolina Symphony.

But when it comes to covering orchestral music in America, what's a fact among reporters? While this error was relatively mild in the grand scheme of things, there is so much unfair and unbalanced reporting going on that one wonders if these reporters are simply copying each other's articles without even applying the integrity of a Google search to their fact-checking.

A recent article in *USA Today* had the web headline "Performing arts face strikes, layoffs, bankruptcy" and the print edition sub-headline read: "Strikes, money woes leave symphonies, operas out of tune." To my knowledge, there was not an orchestra anywhere in the world on strike the day that article was published, but people in hotel lobbies and airport bathrooms (or wherever it is that people read *USA Today*) had the negative perception of symphonic music reinforced by a false headline. I guarantee that most people saw only the headline and didn't bother to read the article. I doubt I would have read it if I hadn't been quoted.

Mark Twain said "There are laws to protect the freedom of the press's speech, but none that are worth anything to protect the people from the press."

It isn't fair of me to blame the press entirely, though. There is no doubt that such inaccurate, negative reporting undermines the success of our organizations, and strengthens the resolve of managements and boards that seek to diminish the presence of our orchestras in their communities. But some of this artless reporting is a result of the industry's self-inflicted wounds. Still, reporters and editors should be more responsible with fact-checking and in offering their readers a less prejudiced, more balanced perspective.

On February 4, *Mother Jones* published perhaps the worse article I've seen. The writer was encouraged by other interviewees to reach out to ICSOM, but she did not. If she had, we might have spared her the indignity of publishing an article so fraught with factual errors that it is certain to be a stain on her journalistic career.

The sub headline of the *Mother Jones* article stated "With lockouts, deficits, and dwindling audiences, classical ensembles fight for survival."

Let's do a little bit of fact-checking on that headline by looking at "dwindling audiences" in 2012, the year that NPR questioned if American orchestras had "hit the wall":

- The Utah Symphony: 23% rise in ticket sales
- The Cleveland Orchestra: on track to set season ticket sales records
- The Cincinnati Symphony: two years of increased attendance
- The St. Louis Symphony: highest ticket sales for December in a decade
- The Buffalo Philharmonic: highest number of subscriptions in its history
- The Oregon Symphony: increase in ticket sales of 19%
- The San Diego Symphony: ticket sales reach an all-time high
- The Kansas City Symphony: ticket sales revenue increased 46.8%

So, why isn't the press writing about the resurgence of attendance for orchestras?

What frustrates me so profoundly is that even when I give reporters positive information, complete with links to support my assertions, most still won't print these facts. So ingrained is the negative outlook, so often from within the field itself, that reporters can only continue to print the same old negative clichés. If the facts don't support the clichés, the facts are discarded.

When I speak about the positive statistics for orchestras, some bloggers and commentators mischaracterize my words by claiming that I am saying that everything is fine and that there is no need to examine the future. Of course, that is not what I am saying at all. I am an advocate for change, though at times it feels like no one is listening. We must reach out to new audiences and new donors. We must learn from the industries that have mastered marketing in the digital age, and we must develop better platforms for social media. Part of the recent success in Cleveland has come from reaching out to new audiences through social media, and as a result of a concerted effort, they have increased their Facebook followers by 16,000 in just nine months, accompanied by a surge in student attendees at Severance Hall.

A Pew Charitable Trusts survey recently reported that "the internet and social media are integral to the arts in America" and the Americans for the Arts *ARTSblog* concluded that "the new and innovative solutions social media offers to the arts is unparalleled."

Our field must change. We must develop new marketing strategies, and we must stop recklessly causing self-inflicted wounds that undermine all we should seek to achieve. Remember that most negative commentators are selling a product, and the product is usually themselves. Not all, but many of them are self-promoters—selling courses, books, or consultancies. The negativity they articulate leaks into the press, where uninformed reporters simply take what they are given, and generally report the loudest voices. But this negativity is cultivating panic, and when those who promote panic are also profiting from it, their message is usually false.

This leads us to the myth of the graying audience—perhaps the single most repeated and unchallenged tenet of the doctrine of failure that undermines success for orchestras. Those who promote this idea look back to audience studies from 1940 that demonstrated the median age of audiences for orchestras was around thirty at that time. They cite statistics through Baumol through recent NEA studies that show, due to aging audiences, we are surely doomed.

But I maintain that if the graying audience is a fact at all, it is being misinterpreted.

In 1940, the average life expectancy in America was 62 years. In 2013, it is 79 years. Never in history has a civilization seen such a rapid increase in life expectancy as in the past century. As a result, the audience for absolutely everything is aging. If you allow me to ignore the increase in life expectancy the way proponents of the myth of the graying audience do, I could make an argument that the audience for *Dora the Explorer* is aging.

Even as the management of the Atlanta Symphony prepared to lock out its musicians, it stated "there is a myth that our audience is old and dwindling." By their own estimation, attendance in Atlanta has been growing at 3% per year, and the average age has dropped from 57 to 52.

While I am constantly encouraged by the many young attendees I see in concert halls across America, I also generally accept that people tend to turn towards attending orchestral concerts as they age, having achieved a measure of success in life that allows them more freedom and leisure time. If that is the case, the fact that we have an opportunity to reach out to that segment of our audiences for an additional 15 years of life expectancy is not a problem—it is an opportunity.

We all must change. We must abandon the new model of failed rhetoric, pathetic media relationships, Boulwaristic lockouts, ineffective marketing, negative pronouncements from self-serving commentators, and the promulgation of the myth of the graying audience.

Observers of recent events can reasonably conclude that the field's manner of training and hiring managers is inherently flawed. That is the new model we must find. How do we train and encourage visionary and charismatic managers, and how do we find them outside of traditional industry searches that have clearly grown ineffective?

It is true that orchestral music has faced a crisis, just as nearly every field has in the economic downturn. But the story to be told is how resilient orchestras have proven to be. The story that reporters should be writing is not that some orchestras have suffered, but rather that so many are reaching new heights. Sometimes, I marvel that any orchestra has remained in business, withstanding the crisis that exists in arts management. Ultimately, as I play for thousands of school children each season, or feel the reaction of an audience to Sibelius or Beethoven, or see the outpouring of love for the locked-out musicians in the Twin Cities, I know orchestras survive because of an increasing relevancy to a society that seeks meaning and comfort in a world that too often slumps with the weight of its burdens.

Microcosms of the Great Divide

SENZA SORDINO
JUNE, 2013

In a time when we all are confronted with a daily onslaught of pessimism, some good news could be found in the release of the Business Committee for the Arts (BCA) *National Survey of Business Support for the Arts*, conducted by our friends at Americans for the Arts, which found that arts contributions continue to recover from the depths of the recession.

From 2009 to 2012, corporate giving to the arts increased by 18%, and the number of businesses that give to the arts increased from 28% to 41%. The median contribution is also the largest it has been in six years, and 17% of the businesses that support the arts expect their giving to increase in the next year.

Still, within our field, there remains great resistance from many managers and boards to the idea that recovery for our orchestras can even be contemplated, and the refrain "our community cannot support a great symphony orchestra" is repeated thoughtlessly in city after city.

Peter Pastreich was recently quoted in the *New York Times* saying: "If I dropped in on the United States from Mars and heard, 'What a disaster!,' what would I see?...Every little town has an orchestra....There are so many places with really dynamic stuff going on. The trouble does not reflect itself in the concert hall. This is an amazingly vibrant musical life."

So why is there so much resistance in discussing the fundraising potential for our orchestras? As I travel, I can't help but feel that our organizations are microcosms of the great divide that has engulfed our nation in the past decade.

I certainly don't mean to suggest that this great divide is necessarily new. After all, any reading of American political history reveals personal assaults from campaigns in the 1800's that make the mechanizations of today's media attacks seem almost quaint. But what is different is that the chasm has now been widened and deepened by unchallenged media platforms where people are making money (and lots of it) to capitalize on the differences we feel as humans.

We live in a political world where people are expected to choose sides and labels. We are "conservative" or we are "liberal." Entire cable networks are devoted to advancing the conservative or liberal ideology under the guise of "news." Well-paid pundits and spokespersons are dispatched with the directive to remain unconvinced by any alternate argument, unmoved by any opponent's logic, and un-swayed by any notion that solutions can sometimes be found in compromise.

Never heard in these so-called debates on Fox News or MSNBC (or others) is the phrase "that's interesting. I never thought about it like that before"—even though learning from each other is one of the essential experiences of life. The polarizing views can loosely be described as representing a largely wealthy, older, and right-leaning class which stands in contrast to a largely underpaid, younger, and left-leaning working class.

The chasm grows through the daily messages of inflexible ideology, and the nation suffers as a result.

Our orchestras are also pervasively experiencing this disconnect in our internal relationships. Our organizations are run by boards who are largely (not entirely) wealthy, older and right-leaning, and those boards depend on the work of a largely (not entirely) underpaid, left-leaning working class. And of course, that working class is unionized, and in many cases the wealthier class is anti-union by political philosophy.

So as the divide has grown in our nation, it has been magnified within our organizations, tiny as they are when compared to great networks or corporations. As a result, in some cases the seemingly inherent and different ideologies of the boards that support our orchestras and the musicians without whom the orchestras would have no means of existence have created dysfunctional microcosms of the great divide.

How does an organization bridge such a chasm? What accounts for the many orchestras that have done remarkably well since the economic downturn, demonstrating that orchestras have proven time and time again to be resilient? Why would a board cling to the notion that fundraising is impossible in this climate even though such a viewpoint requires dismissing the success of other arts organizations?

The answer surely lies in leadership. In our organizations, the fulcrum between the divide must be a manager who can bring people together through charisma, skill, and intelligence. A manager must resist exploiting and deepening the differences of opinions found within the organizations they seek to lead.

So much ink and time is spent on the notion of a "new business model" for our field, but some basic aspects of any successful business are being ignored in the discussion. A successful business knows to protect its "brand" at all costs, and activities that are not central to its mission can only be supported through the strength and recognition of that brand.

For orchestras, our business "brand" is the "product" on stage. Should that brand not be protected through investment, then all other outreach activities are being built on quicksand.

Recently, a managerial leader stated in the *New York Times* that "Success today is not limited to the quality of execution…the things that represent quality today are much more varied, more democratic, more inclusive. Orchestras have to be more innovative, experimental and creative, more advanced in the ways they use technology."

While it is certainly hard to argue with the obvious need for our orchestras to enter the 21st century in our understanding of the opportunities technology presents when it comes to marketing and fundraising, I think it is a mistake to de-emphasize the importance of "quality of execution." Indeed, that is the "brand" without which our organizations have no foundation to build upon, whether that means building educational outreach, or a new lobby.

In the new BCA National Survey, a very relevant fact should be noted and contemplated by all who seek to support arts institutions. Nearly 6 in 10 of the businesses that give to the arts stated that the arts must show a proven need before they will increase their contribution. That is critical. I have said before that people, and businesses, will give to organizations that inspire them, but they will not give to organizations that question their own sustainability. Fundraising, like so many other things, is dependent on inspiration. It is also apparent that it depends on the ability to articulate need. Our field is failing both tests

The messages in our glossy brochures too often conflict with the messages in our inky newspapers. The negativity is soul-crushing, and it is also contribution-killing. We must, as a field, find a way to articulate that not only can our orchestras be saved, but there are reasons to save them. It is through inspiration that we can bridge the great divide.

All the News That Fits the Print:
The Failure of Arts Journalism
at a Time of Cultural Need

WWW.ICSOM.ORG
OCTOBER 10, 2013

October 1 was a difficult day for the musicians of the Minnesota Orchestra, a day that marked the one-year point of the managerial imposed lockout that has silenced an orchestra once called "the best in the world." That morning, their beloved Music Director, Osmo Vanska, delivered his resignation, precisely as he said he would if the lockout did not end. The relationship between Vanska and these musicians had begun to reach the status of legend; a unique pairing of leader and orchestra that had the potential to approach Szell and Cleveland, Ormandy and Philadelphia. So, on this dark morning the Locked Out Musicians of the Minnesota Orchestra did the only thing they knew how, and the only thing their years of dedicated study and training would allow them to do—they went out and served their community.

That morning, those heavy-hearted musicians performed a free concert for school children at a high school in Minnetonka, Minnesota. As the high school's website described the event, it was a concert "for educational purposes meant to enlighten orchestra and band students at Hopkins High School."

But as the musicians gave the very best of themselves that morning, a writer in Britain was preparing to dump his very worst on the world through drivel that a major newspaper, *The Telegraph*, would actually publish even though it would likely have failed a third-grade writing

assignment. As those musicians performed selflessly in a high school auditorium, *The Telegraph* was putting ink to fish wrap with words describ-
ing the musicians as "greedy, complacent, gilded, spoiled, and princely".
Harsh words to be directed at people who haven't received a paycheck in
over a year because their management sought to fix a hole in the roof by
burning down the house.

The writer goes on to offer an analysis of the American orchestral
scene as he sees it, which is apparently through a blindfold. "In recent
years, there has been a spiraling of salaries, and only the stark fact of
mounting deficits has brought some orchestras to their senses." To prove
his point, he cites the Los Angeles Philharmonic, saying "Take the Los
Angeles Philharmonic, the richest of the lot" and he assails the increasing
salaries there "as an astonishing sum."

It is true that the musicians of the Los Angeles Philharmonic are paid
in accordance with professionals who have reached the top of their field,
but it is also true that the organization has achieved a surplus in ten of the
past eleven years. There is no "mounting deficit" in the writer's example,
but I don't mean to confuse him with facts.

This isn't meant to dispute that the week of October 1 was a tough
week. It was heartbreaking in many ways. The resignation of Osmo
Vanska was reported on the same day that the New York City Opera announced it would be filing for bankruptcy. That legendary organization,
dubbed "The People's Opera" by none other than Fiorello La Guardia, had
served the people of New York for 70 years, and its loss is a bitter occur-
rence, but not an unexpected one. The company has been struggling for
a number of years, exacerbated by a terrible managerial decision to move
the opera out of its newly renovated theater at Lincoln Center in 2011.

The bad news from these situations dominated arts journalism.
Apparently, there are some reporters who tend to like stories that don't
require the intensive research of a Google search. These events led to
headlines such "Classical Music's Hell Week" and "It's Been a Really Bad
Week for Classical Music" and of course, the execrable "US Orchestras
are Greedy and Overpaid."

But there was other news that week, though you had to dig pretty
furiously to find it (and after reading the articles referenced above, furious
was my mood.)

- The St. Louis Symphony announced that its revenue had climbed 7%
- The Houston Symphony announced a third year of balanced budgets on the heels of record breaking fundraising, with the most successful annual fund campaign in its 100 year history. Subscription sales to new subscribers so far this season are 70 percent ahead of this point last season.
- The Detroit Symphony announced a 43% jump in fund-raising which led to a record $18.9 million in contributions to the annual fund.

But these items received nary a mention in the national or international press.

Maybe the most troubling example of the failure of arts journalism came from National Public Radio (NPR) on October 5. It was intensely disappointing, and one musician confided in me that he actually threw his radio out the window after he listened to the dramatic misinterpretations and oversimplifications that were spread to a national audience.

The summary of the story promised that NPR would "sort through the wreckage" and explain "why (these) problems represent a larger and more troubling trend" for classical music.

Of course, the feature shed no light on any wreckage, and explained absolutely nothing. But it did fill four minutes of airtime, which apparently was its main purpose.

Perhaps musicians find the faulty reporting on NPR most disturbing because we generally respect the network so much. NPR aspires to a higher ideal, and when they fail to reach that height, it disappoints. In this case it barely seemed like they were trying.

In the October 5 NPR story, two on-air personalities analyzed the developing "wreckage" of classical music with such profound expressions as "Yikes!" In fact, "Yikes" was so profound they used it twice. (After all, the format does provide for extended coverage.)

"Yeah. Yikes. I mean, I feel like it's a week when the classical music world tried to one-up Congress and the government shutdown."

The unlistenable banter focused on three (and only three) events:

- The Minnesota Orchestra situation
- The New York City Opera bankruptcy, which really "bums (them) out."
- The strike at Carnegie Hall by Local 1 IATSE Stagehands that cancelled a Philadelphia Orchestra performance

What does a strike by stagehands, totally out of the control of any orchestra, have to do with anything? In fact, the commentators could have used it as evidence of the flexibility and commitment of orchestral musicians to their communities, as the musicians of the Philadelphia Orchestra worked quickly and cooperatively with their management, waiving multiple contractual issues, to allow for a free "pop-up" concert back home in Philadelphia that played to a full hall, even though it was announced at the last minute. That is the positive orchestral story to come from the IATSE strike. But no, the generosity and dedication of those musicians didn't fit the script that NPR had in mind.

But worst of all, NPR provided a microphone for the analysts to refer to the yellowest of journalism, the aforementioned and dismissed piece from *The Telegraph*.

"I don't know if you read. There's a very interesting article in *The Telegraph* this past week, the London paper, from Ivan Hewitt, a classical music critic. He was extremely blunt, saying that U.S. orchestra musicians are grossly overpaid and greedy."

I want to assure all British musicians that the musicians of American orchestras will always be their advocates, and we will always praise their artistry as we seek to assist them in bettering their livelihoods. Their positions cannot be improved by attacking ours.

In all of these stories, the illusion of fairness could have been created by reporting a story that I can only dream about. What if instead we were to read:

> "The Minnesota Orchestra situation is a tragedy for the community, and the loss of the New York City Opera marks the end of a grand era for the company. But the news is largely good in this climate for classical music. Orchestras in Dallas, Los Angeles, Baltimore, Pittsburgh

and Washington DC all settled contracts quite amicably and with modest gains for the musicians. Arts giving is making a healthy recovery from the recession, orchestras are innovatively reaching out to larger audiences with new technologies, and the cautionary tales from Minnesota can be utilized by a field that seeks to preserve a great tradition as it reaches an expanding audience that benefits economically, spiritually, educationally, and in issues of personal health from exposure to music."

But that is not what we read. Oscar Wilde said that "In old days men had the rack. Today they have the press."

I am not just a critic of arts journalism; I want to help. For their next articles, journalists might explore these facts:

- In 2012, philanthropic giving to the arts in America reached an all-time high of $14.4 billion dollars
- In the past three years, the number of businesses giving to the arts increased by 18%
- 17% of businesses that give to the arts say they plan to increase their giving next year
- Philanthropic giving to the arts is recovering from the recession at twice the rate of other philanthropic giving
- The arts in America are a healthy business, leading to over 4 million jobs and providing over $135 billion in economic activity.

In Cleveland, the number of students attending concerts in Severance Hall has doubled. The Chicago Lyric Opera saw an increase in attendance last year of 15%. In 2012, the Kansas City Symphony saw an increase in ticket revenues of over 46%, along with record attendance. The San Diego Symphony has seen a decade of balanced finances even as it more than doubled its budget. The Buffalo Philharmonic sold more subscriptions than at any point in its 75-year history.

The true story to be told is how well orchestras have weathered the recession, demonstrating once again the viability of our nation's artistic organizations.

There are great arts journalists that still exist, and there is great analysis being written, but part of the problem has been that as newspapers have reduced their arts coverage, the most knowledgeable writers have lost their positions. A few years ago I delivered a speech in which I said:

> "We must continue to build our relationships with the press. As we ask those who cover us to be our advocates, we must be their advocates as well. In too many cities we see our print media outlets eliminating their music critics and arts editors. No newspaper can adequately serve their community without devoting coverage to the local and national arts scene."

In our instant media world, that is truer now than ever. Musicians must be advocates for arts journalists, just as we are advocates for every aspect of our great communities. When a false and negative message is reported at the expense of the positive message that will serve the next generation of Americans through a commitment to our cultural institutions, we must respond.

I am occasionally criticized for being too positive about the future of the arts, and I am proud to wear that criticism as a badge of honor. Certain bloggers will twist my words to fit into their negative message of self-promotion, and that's fine. But readers have a right to know that false statements such as "(Minneapolis is) the only city supporting two professional orchestras" will be challenged by writers who will commit to at least a minimum of research.

The famous slogan of the *New York Times* is "All the News That's Fit to Print." Unfortunately for many press outlets, when it comes to reporting on classical music it would be more accurate to say "all the news that fits the print." Too often, positive facts are discarded if they don't fit the century-old narrative of the impending death of classical music. If one were to believe the negative messages found in the media about orchestras, you might be led to question the validity of hope.

The good news I bring you is that the bad news that permeates so many discussions of the future is largely false. Unfortunately though, such false messages can be self-fulfilling, and we must not allow our resolve to be repelled by an assault of damaging words. Still, we have no claim to condemn the negative messages about our orchestras if we are not doing everything we can to disclaim them. As musicians, we cannot allow destructive messages to undermine our idealism and hope. The comfort we take comes from the indisputable truth that the positive message offered by musicians will far outlast the negativity of those that misrepresent us.

Highway 23 Revisited: A look back at ICSOM's keynote address at the University of Michigan

SENZA SORDINO
MAY, 2014

Recently I was speaking with a group of young musicians preparing to embark upon their professional careers. We were covering many of the issues that symphonic musicians must confront and exploring the important role that advocacy will play for the next generation of orchestral players. Of course, the musicians were interested in the recent, well-publicized difficulties in the field, such as last season's spate of lockouts. I told them that, in my experience, virtually every such problem could be anticipated and avoided. I was asked, "How could the Minnesota Orchestra lockout have been anticipated?"

The question made me revisit a keynote address I delivered at the University of Michigan on March 22, 2012, titled *Danger, Will Robinson! How Hyperbolic, Negative Rhetoric is Hurting America's Orchestras*. The speech was part of the University of Michigan's American Orchestra Summit II, and my remarks caused a bit of discomfort at the event. The address was circulated widely on the Internet, receiving both criticism and praise. I felt on the day I delivered the address that it was my proudest moment as ICSOM chair, and two years later that feeling has grown.

It was not an easy speech to deliver. It was 45 minutes of analysis, and while the focus of the speech was to engage the field in more positive messaging, it did contain some pointed criticism. Historically, the many calls for change in our field have never been met with actual change in the tone of the dialogue. I felt that the time was right for this speech, and since I had been offered this forum, I felt obliged to stand up and make some challenging statements. I was excited and honored when I read reports later that called the speech both "controversial" and "courageous."

I made a lot of observations and predictions in that speech, and to both my satisfaction and dissatisfaction, revisiting the address shows that time has proved the statements correct.

> *Right now, at this very moment, there are orchestra managements preparing their organizations for extended and unnecessary work stoppages. One in particular will be prominently in the press as early as this fall, but I don't want to name the organization as I have hope that the management will avoid this destructive path. There is still time. But resources spent in this direction are also resources that could be spent promoting their organization.*

Immediately following the speech, I received inquiries from the Minneapolis press to inquire if I was speaking of the Minnesota Orchestra. While I avoided those questions at the time, it was pretty clear that I was. This statement turned out to be even more accurate than I anticipated. Not only was the Minnesota management preparing for an extended lockout of unprecedented length, but the musicians of Indianapolis, Atlanta, and Saint Paul would also face lockouts. All were foreseeable and avoidable.

> *The musicians of Syracuse will accomplish what their former management could not, and I have no doubt an orchestra will re-emerge.*

Since the board of the Syracuse Symphony filed for Chapter 7 liquidation in 2011 (an action I labeled "preventable" at the time in the Syracuse *Post-Standard*), the musicians of the orchestra have taken up the mantle, and great orchestral music has returned to Central New York in the form of Symphoria. While a lot of work remains to ensure the success of this spectacular effort, the musicians are on the path to success by moving in a direction of positive advocacy that their previous management refused even to acknowledge.

> *In Louisville, an orchestra that has commissioned 120 original compositions and performed over 400 world premieres which served to spread the music of America across the globe is currently functioning as an organization that employs no musicians. It is an orchestra built by the people and led at its founding by a mayor who believed in the concept of Confucianism that said that a city of high culture with happy citizens will attract wealth, business and power to the city. But now, this historic orchestra looks for musicians on Craigslist and through Facebook ads.*

The promise of the Louisville Orchestra has been renewed since the time of this speech. The efforts by the previous manager and board president to replace the musicians failed. ICSOM issued statements that spread around the world in 24 hours, urging musicians and teachers to ignore the bogus calls for applications through Craigslist. Today, the Louisville Orchestra moves forward with a new CEO, a new board chair, a new music director, and a new president of their local union, all brought about through the extraordinary dedication and perseverance of the musicians of the orchestra.

Regarding media, I said:

> *Another manager has challenged the jurisdiction of national media contracts, appealing their lost case numerous times and spending who knows how much in legal fees. That money could have funded multiple projects that would have elevated the organization in the mind of the local and international community. Instead, money raised from donors has gone to lawyers.*

Following the Michigan event, the management's appeal was lost again.

I also issued some criticisms of the League of American Orchestras, specifically about their programming for the 2012 League Conference:

I have expressed my concern to the leadership of the League that their programming may be viewed as negative by musicians, and that the chasm may well widen.

On this point, I wish I had not been correct. The chasm has indeed widened, and that is regrettable.

Referencing negative statements by board members, I said:

The leadership of the League must speak out against such destructiveness, and when they do not, it weakens the organization in the eyes of musicians and managers alike.

Regrettably, the League remained silent throughout the Minnesota Orchestra lockout.

[I]n my writings I have called on musicians to avoid casting aspersions towards the League, and I have asked the League to issue similar statements to its members about the way they regard their musicians. While I've yet to hear my public appeal matched, I remain hopeful.

We have yet to hear similar public calls for a change in tone from the League leadership. But that could change. In fact, organizations with differences of opinion can always find ways to work together on shared goals. As we face some difficulties for musicians over the issue of the ban issued by the U.S. Fish and Wildlife Service on items containing ivory, we would like to acknowledge the efforts put in to this issue by Heather Noonan, the League's vice president for advocacy in Washington, D.C. Musicians everywhere should thank her for her work, and we hope to find ways to work together in this effort to protect endangered species while also providing guidance and security for musicians and their instruments.

As ICSOM led at its founding, we intend to lead again into a new era of positive advocacy. To musicians everywhere, I call on you to join us in our positive message of advocacy. It is not enough to simply play your instrument. You must be among your audience, out in the lobby of your concert hall. Shake the hands of your audiences, thank your donors, and welcome them into an environment of community that surrounds every orchestra.

Since this speech, ICSOM celebrated its 50th anniversary in Chicago. Our members have clearly taken a greater role in advocacy, with the musicians of nearly every member orchestra now spreading their positive message through social networking and meeting with their patrons in the lobbies of their concert halls. Many positive things have occurred for the field, and I do think the dialogue has improved.

However, a few destructive things have happened as well, and Minnesota must serve as a cautionary tale for us all. The actions of the board and management during the lockout there were despicable, and no one in this field can afford to stand silent at such disrespect to the music of Beethoven and the people of our communities.

> We must harvest the frustration that we all are feeling and use it as inspiration….We must be inspired by the challenge. And we must not hesitate to dream great dreams simply because they are hard to achieve….This is our mission, and we must join together as never before, because something precious is at stake.

The conclusion of the speech remains true for me as well, and as I meet with even more musicians, managers, patrons, board leaders, and journalists, my optimism for the next generation grows.

> This judgment we make affirmatively: if we can change the tone, then we can change the future.

A Teacher Remembered

INTERNATIONAL MUSICIAN
JUNE, 2014

A few evenings ago, I left the stage after Mahler's Third Symphony and found a message waiting for me with the news that Carroll Bailey, Sr. had died at the age of 91. I could not help but slump in tears.

Mr. Bailey was my first bass teacher, and without him I would not have become a musician, and I certainly wouldn't be Chair of ICSOM. He might not have been famous, but for the many lives he touched he should be remembered throughout the music world.

He was a peaceful man who came from sturdy Midwestern roots. After moving to Virginia, Mr. Bailey first played the trumpet, performing jazz in the Tidewater area with such notables as Portsmouth native Tommy Newsom.

Local 125 president John Lindberg once said that Mr. Bailey could play "any melody, in any key, from memory."

Mr. Bailey became principal trumpet of the Virginia Symphony (then known as the Norfolk Symphony.) After suffering an embouchure injury, he adeptly switched to the bass, which he had been practicing for some time. He said "When I got to the string bass I fell in love with it like it had been waiting for me for years." He performed with the orchestra for more than 50 years, and even into his late 80's practiced every day "just for the love of it."

Mr. Bailey took me to my first union meeting, at Local 125 in Norfolk, when I was just 15 years old. He taught me to respect music, and to respect musicians. He introduced me to the traditions of the field, corrected my youthful mistakes with care, and admonished my youthful indiscretions with compassion. He told me that I was too concerned with "fast fingers" and impressing people, and not concerned enough with "playing beautifully." He bought me a book of song melodies and told me to just play them, and no other etudes, until it was the melody that I loved most. Apparently satisfied with my effort, he welcomed me as his colleague within barely a year of our first lesson.

Countless studies indicate that music is key to a child's development. Those of you who are teaching now surely must understand the important roles you have in your students' lives. But all of us who have reached some level of success know a teacher with whom we have an everlasting bond, who taught us something that we seek to keep alive in our playing every day. That is what I lost the other evening. Mr. Bailey was a happy and content man who was aware that he had lived a very honorable life. But for me, I lost a connection to my youth and to those first moments when I knew nothing of the negativity that sometimes surrounds our field, and when every note I was hearing and playing was new and amazing. Like Mr. Bailey once said "I haven't found one piece of music I didn't end up liking."

I was also sad that I had not seen him recently, with my work and travels so all-consuming. The last time I spoke to him I told him "I always thought you were the greatest teacher I ever had Mr. Bailey." I wish I could have told him that one last time.

For those of you fortunate enough to still have your first teacher, give them a call. Let them know what you are doing, and let them know the important roles they played in your life.

Tonight I will play Mahler's Third Symphony again with my always inspiring colleagues in the North Carolina Symphony. I will be remembering my earliest lessons, and I hope I can honor Mr. Bailey by keeping his joyful love of music in my playing.

Sowing the Wind

SENZA SORDINO
AUGUST, 2014

We have often marveled (and occasionally despaired) at the fact that we work in a field where all too often organizational failure is accepted, and all too often such failure is even expected. This has never been more strikingly illustrated than in the recent announcement from the management of the Green Bay Symphony that it would close following the 2014–2015 season despite several recent profitable years.

The executive director publicly labeled the profitable years "a fluke." What other business would do that? Well—no other business. It is just too bizarre. Successful businesses would highlight the profits, knowing that success breeds success. No business would dismiss profits as a fluke, thereby suggesting that their successes had nothing to do with the quality of the product, the excellence of the employees, or the importance of the service to the community.

The Green Bay Symphony website's home page currently trumpets "GBSO's Farewell Season!" That's right—there really is an exclamation point. The text audaciously goes on to say, "Join us as we celebrate the tradition of great music!" The management seems pretty excited about giving up on a 100-year legacy where the citizens of the community and the great musicians of the orchestra clearly deserve better. The website also asks, "Why should a community support an orchestra that's in its final season?" Actually, that is a pretty good question.

I want to go a little easy on my criticism, though, as it seems apparent that this orchestra can be saved, and hopefully people with wisdom can be found in the community to recover from this fell proclamation, and the orchestra can be led with vision into its next century. I do not desire that my comments poison that well.

But in a field where failure it too often accepted, even expected, it seems amazing that so many orchestras can overcome such suppositions and perform so well, especially in these economic times. Such successes are being experienced in places with positive expectations, and in life what you expect is often what you will get. If you find failure to be a reasonable result, and you spread such a message, then negative results are often what your vision will deliver.

For they sow the wind, and they shall reap the whirlwind.

As we review the orchestral season, it is clear that difficulties remain, and clearer still that there are a few storms ahead. But what is even more apparent is that, if success is a fluke, there certainly have been a lot of "fluky" things going on for orchestras and the arts.

- The Chicago Symphony received the two largest gifts in its history, totaling $32 million.
- The Indianapolis Symphony saw a 19% surge in ticket sales with an increase of 30% in subscription sales.
- The Cleveland Orchestra announced a balanced budget, growing audiences, increased endowment, and a record number of student attendees.
- The Houston Grand Opera received a $750,000 grant to assist in producing new works, while also achieving record attendance and fundraising.
- The Arizona Opera erased its debt.
- The Lyric Opera of Chicago, which has operated in the black for 26 of the past 27 seasons, saw significant increases in revenue and fundraising, and an increase of 8% in ticket sales.
- New York City increased funding for arts in the public schools by $23 million and is expected to hire 120 additional arts teachers.
- As Symphoria works heroically to establish a permanent orchestral presence in Syracuse in the wake of the unnecessary Syracuse Symphony bankruptcy, the new orchestra is now receiving grants, including funding for its educational mission.

- The San Antonio Symphony celebrated its 75th anniversary as it prepares to move into its new home, the Tobin Center.
- The Florida Orchestra saw an increase in attendance of 30%.
- The Houston Symphony's gala raised over $2.5 million in one evening for education programs.
- The New York City Ballet's Spring Gala celebrated 50 years at Lincoln Center and raised $3.15 million.
- The Milwaukee Symphony reached a goal of $5 million from new donors.
- The Cincinnati Symphony's endowment has grown by 43%, and the number of gifts has increased by 94%, leading to a double-digit increase in attendance.
- The Grand Rapids Symphony launched a $40 million endowment drive with a $20 million gift.
- The Detroit Symphony's holiday concerts set a new box office record.
- The Buffalo Philharmonic saw an increase in concert revenue of 5.5%, an 11.9% surge in contributions, endowment growth of 7.7%, and an increase in ticket sales with records set for subscriptions.

I have been traveling the world over the past decade spreading the message that for every story of failure there are ten stories of success for the arts, all the while hoping that we could sow the seeds of positive advocacy that could lead to a new era of artistic relevance for the modern world. I was recently inspired by a quote from Gustav Mahler, who said, "I am hitting my head against the walls, but the walls are giving way."

Yes, there were some bad stories this year, too, and there will be others. That's how life is. There is good and there is bad. It is true for orchestras just as it is true for every other type of business. It has been reported that 90% of restaurants in America fail in their first year of business, yet no one would argue that Americans no longer like to eat.

Results aren't always a fluke. Sometimes success is the result of hard work, cooperative and visionary thinking, mutual respect, and positive expectations. I do not doubt, even for one second, the importance of our orchestras or our ability to succeed as we continue on as a beacon for a world that longs for light and inspiration. There is nothing negative about what we do. We teach the next generation. We serve our communities. We constantly aspire for something greater than ourselves.

We play music.

Lockout, Rinse, Repeat

SENZA SORDINO
DECEMBER 2014

On August 25, 2012, the management of the Atlanta Symphony Orchestra and the Board of the Woodruff Arts Center locked out the musicians of the Atlanta Symphony.

On September 7, 2014, the management of the Atlanta Symphony Orchestra and the Board of the Woodruff Arts Center locked out the musicians of the Atlanta Symphony.

In an often misattributed and perhaps apocryphal quote, it has been opined that the definition of insanity is doing the same thing over and over and expecting different results.

The Atlanta Symphony lockout of 2012 brought negative attention to that great city, and temporarily silenced one of ICSOM's finest orchestras. It brought division and mistrust to the organization, laying a negative foundation for relationships among all facets of the institution.

So naturally, seeing those results, the board thought they'd go back for seconds, and the 2014 lockout would last over two months.

Musicians and arts enthusiasts all over the world followed the events in Atlanta, and we are all relieved that this second lockout is over. May it be the last time that an orchestra faces such a destructive tactic. The settlement that has been reached could have been achieved by continuing the negotiations and following the musicians' call to play and talk, leading to the same conclusion without ever missing a concert and without damaging the brand of the orchestra with yet another lockout.

While many of our orchestras are achieving great things, it is difficult to hear the great results over the din of self-fulfilling negativity that emanates when a lockout is inflicted upon an orchestra and a community. And there have been too many lockouts recently: Minnesota Orchestra, Saint Paul Chamber Orchestra, Indianapolis Symphony, the Atlanta Symphony, and...the Atlanta Symphony.

We hear so much talk about business models, but what is so obviously lost in that discussion is one basic fact: lockouts are bad business. Lockouts bring negative international attention to the community, undermine the confidence of donors, and reinforce negative stereotypes about the future of the arts.

We noted at the start of the 2014 ICSOM Conference in Los Angeles that for the first time in several years we were commencing our discussions on a day on which no orchestra was locked out. But we also noted that we didn't know what would happen even in the next few weeks. We praised the overwhelming and uplifting response from our members to ICSOM's Calls to Action to assist our members in need, while noting that as uplifting as the response to these Calls to Action has been, we nonetheless hope we never have to issue another.

But we know we will, and we know we must remain prepared to support any musician in need.

In the weeks immediately following the 2014 ICSOM Conference, Atlanta was locked out...again. We issued a Call to Action, and immediately our members, and our friends across the continent, responded. In less than one month, it became the third most successful Call to Action we have ever issued. In those moments when we feel discouraged by the negativity that sometimes surrounds our field, we should take comfort in the fact that the musicians of ICSOM will always stand together, and will always be eager to assist each other.

While positive news inevitably receives less media coverage, events outside of Atlanta have occurred as well since the conclusion of the 2014 ICSOM Conference. At a time when the leaders at the Woodruff Arts Center were once again laying out the tired and embarrassing rhetoric of the goal to establish a new model for orchestras everywhere; other orchestras were working to achieve different things:

- The San Antonio Symphony celebrated its 75ᵗʰ anniversary by moving into its new concert hall after closing its fiscal year with a surplus and receiving a one million dollar gift.
- The Chicago Symphony gala marked 125 years and raised $1.5 million even as the orchestra reported a fourth year of record sales and fundraising.
- The Detroit Symphony reported that annual giving has surpassed the goal of $17.4 million.
- The Grand Rapids Symphony received a $1 million gift for its endowment.
- The Lyric Opera of Chicago's 60ᵗʰ Anniversary Concert and Diamond Ball raised $3.2 million.
- The Kansas City Symphony achieved international recognition as a symbol of its city with its appearance at Game 6 of the World Series.

As I watched the broadcast of Game 6, filled with pride for all of our friends in the Kansas City Symphony, noting how far we have come in working to brand our member orchestras as indispensable to our communities, I couldn't help but wonder what would have happened had the Atlanta Braves been playing in the 2014 World Series. A moment that the management of the Kansas City Symphony was able to cultivate would have been lost by the management of the Woodruff Arts Center, because they were too busy talking about what was not possible, as opposed to what was achievable.

When we hear the clichéd rhetoric of "new business models," we must always remember and be prepared to articulate that our friends at Americans for the Arts regularly conduct a study called the BCA Survey of Business Support for the Arts. The conclusions of businesses that support the arts include:

- 64% agreed that businesses could also support other social causes by giving to the arts;
- 59% found the arts to have a direct impact on the company's bottom line and a direct tie-in to the company name or products;
- 59% stated that the arts can promote employee creativity and growth.

The theme of the 2014 ICSOM Conference was The Art of Advocacy. It has long been our belief that musicians must be their own most ardent advocates, and throughout ICSOM that is being achieved. Virtually all of our musicians have developed skills at utilizing social networking for positive messaging, and the use of Twitter played a prominent role in avoiding a lockout at the Metropolitan Opera. At our Los Angeles conference, George Brown of the Utah Symphony gave a presentation on the development of a Fourth Wall committee by the musicians of the Utah Symphony, designed to ensure that their positive message about the future of the arts crosses the wall of the stage as clearly as their music.

In Atlanta, the musicians and their committee leadership elevated the art form. Building upon the inspiring efforts of the Met Opera musicians, the Minnesota Orchestra musicians and so many others, the Atlanta Symphony musicians built a social networking campaign that was followed by thousands and thousands. Bloggers from across the world took notice and supported the musicians, analyzing every statement uttered by the Woodruff Arts Center leaders. Financial support from other orchestras rolled in, and pictures of the Boston Symphony, the Cincinnati Symphony, the New York Philharmonic, and others were posted with many of the musicians wearing ATL Symphony Musicians t-shirts.

The Calls to Action that we issue for financial support for musicians facing lockouts always state: "…if we effectively respond to every call, we will demonstrate the power in collective action. We can and will make a powerful statement to our managements and boards as we work to spread the positive community message of the musicians of ICSOM."

Every member of ICSOM can take pride that we once again responded effectively. I am so proud of the musicians of the Atlanta Symphony, and privileged to be associated with all the members of ICSOM.

2014: A Great Year for Orchestras (or haven't you heard?)

METROPOLITAN OPERA
ORCHESTRA MUSICIANS' BLOG
WWW.METORCHESTRAMUSICIANS.ORG
DECEMBER 29, 2014

In almost every article about orchestras, no matter how positive the news being reported might be, there seems to be some obligation to include a sentence that says something along the lines of "this good news is in contrast to the dire situations facing orchestras across the country." Unfortunately, this only serves to emphasize a stereotype that fits into the interminably repeated rhetoric of the "death of classical music."

A recent article in the *Detroit News* reported that the Detroit Symphony just announced its second consecutive year of balanced budgets, and finished this fiscal year with a surplus. The article also reported increased attendance, increased ticket revenue, and an increase in the number of individual donors.

Still, it included the obligatory disclaimer: "Given the miserable environment for orchestras nationwide, this (news) is particularly encouraging."

I would suggest that this miserable environment, so often referenced and unchallenged, is highly exaggerated if it exists at all.

They say that orchestras are dying, but the San Antonio Symphony celebrated its 75th anniversary and moved into its new concert hall, the Tobin Center.

They say that attendance is declining, but the Florida Orchestra saw a 30% increase in attendance, and the Buffalo Philharmonic set a record for subscription sales.

They say that contributions to orchestras are diminishing, but the Los Angeles Philharmonic received a $20 million gift, and the Chicago Symphony received the two largest gifts in its history, totaling over $32 million.

And, they say that audiences are aging, but The Cleveland Orchestra saw paid attendance by college-aged students rise 50 percent, while twice as many attendees were under the age of 18 as in the previous season.

We understand that it is the nature of the press to report negative stories. In fact, reporting on the "death" of institutions across the American landscape is a bit of a pastime. Google "the death of TV", or "the death of film", or even "the death of the NFL" and you'll find rhetoric similar to that used to describe the assumed faltering future of orchestras.

But why does this matter? It is because the greatest threat to a thriving future for the arts in America is the persistent and seemingly unchallenged negative rhetoric about the future of the arts in America.

Despite the tired clichés about the impending demise of classical music, 2014 proved a great year for orchestras.

- The Lyric Opera of Chicago's 60th anniversary concert and Ball raised $3.2 million in one evening, on the heels of an increase in attendance of 15%
- The Grand Rapids Symphony received a $1 million gift for its endowment
- The North Carolina Symphony saw an increase of 40% in attendance for its Summerfest concerts
- The Louisiana Philharmonic raised more than $2 million for a cash reserve fund
- The St. Paul Chamber Orchestra saw a 20-year high in attendance
- The Toronto Symphony reported a budget surplus and increased attendance
- The Buffalo Philharmonic received a substantial gift to endow its Music Director chair
- The Indianapolis Symphony saw an increase in attendance of 18%

- The Houston Symphony raised over $2.5 million in one evening for its educational programs on the heels of four years of record breaking fundraising

In view of these facts, it is hard to understand how anyone would feel obliged to call this "a miserable environment." Such negative coverage, though inevitable owing to the nature of the press that perpetually leads with negatives, undermines our future. But, it is really nothing new. The rhetoric that insists that the sky is falling for orchestras has been around for decades. It has become its own tradition in a field filled with traditions.

An article from United Press International, titled *25 Orchestras Doomed to Die*, forecast the demise of multiple symphony orchestras throughout America. This is quite alarming, except this article was published in 1970, and the predictions have been proven wrong for over forty years.

It went on to say (remember, in 1970) that "orchestras have one alternative to going out of business." They must "reshape - either by reducing the size of orchestras...or by shortening seasons."

Does any of this sound familiar?

We have a document written by the president of the board of the Chicago Symphony, who said:

"The (Chicago Symphony) now must solve a problem which has arisen from economic conditions beyond its control. A deficit has been incurred, and undoubtedly there will be annual deficits for some years to come. This affects the future of the orchestra...Our problem does not differ in kind from the financial problem that faces each of the major orchestras in the United States."

This is especially troubling isn't it?... that an orchestra as great as the Chicago Symphony could face this predicament. I would be more concerned had this not been written in April, 1940.

There is one great sentence in this 1940 document though. In a message that everyone in our field should heed, especially today, the board chair stated:

"We cannot reduce our expenses below our present level without seriously endangering our standard of symphony music, which would soon result in endangering our principal source of income."

None of this is meant to dismiss that there have been difficulties for the field. Just as many businesses suffered from the effects of the 2008 recession, so have orchestras. But the true story to be told is how resilient our orchestras have been in recovering and emerging from the economic downturn. Even some orchestras that sadly had to suspend operations are being revitalized as they reorganize in a more positive environment.

Other businesses suffer similar difficulties. After all, it is said that 90% of restaurants fail in their first year of business, but no one uses that statistic to claim that Americans no longer like to eat.

Some of the successes we are seeing have been made possible by the sacrifices of musicians during difficult times. Now that we are seeing improved finances for many orchestras, sustained growth can only be achieved by reinvesting in the musicians who have demonstrated such dedication to their communities.

The difficulties we have seen speak to the need for a greater investment in our orchestras and the musicians who keep them vital. Our orchestras are among the most prominent artistic institutions in our nation, and the non-profit arts and culture industry in America is a $135 billion dollar business that supports over 4.13 million American jobs. The role of music in education and health is undisputed, and the musicians of our orchestras selflessly serve our communities by enhancing the benefits derived by the presence of a world-class performing arts institution.

Classical performers are everywhere. This year saw Renee Fleming sing before a world-wide audience at the Super Bowl, bringing positive attention to the world of opera. And in October, Joyce DiDonato and the Kansas City Symphony performed before Game 6 of the World Series, demonstrating the indispensable value that orchestra has to its city. People sometimes like to bemoan that there aren't many classical artists on TV, and they point to the fact that Johnny Carson used to occasionally host opera singers and instrumentalists. But how great was it to see Jessye Norman on David Letterman's show on November 21? And his announced successor, Stephen Colbert, has welcomed classical artists on his program over the years including Placido Domingo, Yo-Yo Ma, Philip Glass, Itzhak Perlman, Lorin Maazel and even classical music critic Alex Ross!

In 2014, reports included that the endowment for the St. Louis Symphony rose by $14 million. The Cincinnati Symphony saw a growth in its endowment of 43%, along with a 94% increase in the number of gifts since 2009 and a double-digit increase in attendance. And, the Philadelphia Orchestra reported increased attendance and ticket revenue.

Our orchestras do not exist in a "miserable environment." They exist, and thrive, in an environment of pure inspiration. Surely, some orchestras will encounter difficulties as we move forward, but there will be far more successes, and far more evenings of music that will uplift our audiences, serve the business environment of our nation, and educate the next generation. These are the truths to be told, and these are the truths musicians will continue to tell…both through our music and through our dedication to our communities.

Our Music Is a Statement for Peace

INTERNATIONAL MUSICIAN
FEBRUARY, 2015

On January 7, the world was once again shocked by a despicable act of terrorism, this time on the streets of Paris. And also again, the world turned to music to respond to and attempt to recover from the scenes of hatred, even though it is impossible to make sense of such heinous acts.

In London, 150 musicians gathered to perform Samuel Barber's *Adagio for Strings* in memory of the victims of the attacks in Paris. In New York, the music director of the New York Philharmonic, Alan Gilbert, dedicated a concert to the victims of the attack and to the "fundamental principle of freedom of speech." "For this first concert of 2015, we were hoping to present a program of joyous music that would be possible to enjoy without thinking about the difficulties and troubles in the world," he said. "Unfortunately, that is just not possible."

In Paris, artists would not be silenced, even for a moment, by this assault on free speech. Plans for the opening of the new La Philharmonie, which will be Paris's largest cultural venue, continued without hesitation. Performances by the Orchestre de Paris, the Paris Opera, and the Orchestre Philharmonic de Radio France went forward without interruption, in honor of the victims and in solidarity with the world community.

Opera and orchestra managers across Italy issued a joint statement defending "all the values that are an achievement of our civilization."

In my home orchestra, North Carolina Symphony, our performance of *An American in Paris* was introduced by our guest conductor, Edwin Outwater, who stated, "this week, we are all Americans in Paris."

As Leonard Bernstein famously said just after the assassination of

President Kennedy, "This sorrow and rage will not inflame us to seek retribution; rather they will inflame our art. Our music will never again be quite the same. This will be our reply to violence: to make music more intensely, more beautifully, more devotedly than ever before."

At times of such inexplicable violence, music remains a salve for the world. Our performances across the world are displays of unity, reminding us of the best of the human spirit in moments where our TV screens are filled with images that could make us feel a sense of despair.

As artists, we must never feel such a sense of futility. Every note we play is a proclamation of support for the human race, and every concert we perform is inherently anti-violence and anti-terrorism.

As musicians and artists, we must never remain silent. Our expression of human emotion, both joyful and grief-stricken, is vital for the world.

During World War II, Winston Churchill is reported to have said: "The arts are essential to any complete national life. The state owes it to itself to sustain and encourage them ... ill fares the race which fails to salute the arts with the reverence and delight which are their due."

The Paris attacks were attacks on free speech, and on artists everywhere. In America, where orchestras are now seeing a recovery following the depths of the recession, we have renewed opportunities to serve our communities, to stand for freedom, and to make every performance a declaration of our faith in humanity. These acts will "inflame our art," and renew our commitment to play music "more devotedly than ever before." Every time we walk on stage holding our instruments, we are making a statement for peace.

The Defiant Opera House of Donetsk

SENZA SORDINO
MARCH, 2015

Recent days have seen an intense escalation of the conflict in Ukraine, which began in 2013 and led to a revolt that ousted President Viktor Yanukovich in early 2014. When Russia subsequently annexed Crimea, a war ensued between pro-Russian factions and the government established in Ukraine following Yanukovich's removal from office. The city of Donetsk has taken the brunt of the conflict, with over 5000 deaths on its 236 year-old streets as bombs drop unceasingly and the streets are patrolled by armed men in tanks. Roughly half of the city's citizens have fled.

In the face of this terrible violence, one institution remains defiantly open, the Donetsk Opera House. Built in 1936, the Donetsk Opera and Ballet Theater produced its first opera in 1941 and it survived World War II and the Nazi occupation of the city. The theater has 960 seats, and features a large bust of Alexander Pushkin in its lobby.

In the midst of the conflict, operas are being produced on a weekly basis. Recent productions have included *Eugene Onegin*, *Die Fledermaus*, and *La Traviata*. The artists are putting their lives at risk every time they walk to the theater, as are the audience members who stand in line for free tickets. The operas must be scheduled in the daylight, as nighttime in the city is simply too dangerous.

In a recent article in the *Guardian*, the deputy director of the opera was quoted as saying that for the opening production of this season, "Tickets were free and there were hundreds of people queuing...People were upset they couldn't get in. In the end we had people sitting on the steps, standing in the wings, we crammed in as many as we could. Two old ladies were in tears, on their knees and kissing (the director's) hands in gratitude that he had opened the season."

The violence in the streets led to the cancellation of plans for Donetsk to host the International Ice Hockey Federation World Championships later this spring, but the Opera remains defiant.

The *Guardian* went on to quote baritone Sergei Dubnitsky: "Maybe it sounds pretentious, but I think we have a certain moral obligation to stay", he said. "We have our performances, our audience, our city to think about. You can treat wounds with medicines, but art is medicine for the soul."

It never leaves my thoughts how the world turns constantly to music. On days of joy, such as weddings, our happiness must be accompanied by music. On days of great personal pain, such as memorial services, we must be comforted by music. On regular days, when we need solace from everyday trials, we turn to music. And in times of great tragedy and devastation, music reminds us of the most noble aspirations of humanity as citizens of the world refuse to allow violence to rob us of any part of our souls.

I think of Mstislav Rostropovich playing Bach by the Berlin Wall, and Leonard Bernstein joyously celebrating freedom with Beethoven's Ninth Symphony just after the *Mauerfall*. I'm listening now to my vinyl recording of the Boston Symphony playing Mozart's *Requiem* just after the death of President Kennedy. I remember orchestras across the world performing immediately following September 11, bringing their communities together around music. I am moved at the thought of 150 musicians playing Barber's *Adagio* in Trafalgar Square following the recent terrorist attacks in Paris.

One of the citizens of Donetsk who attended the opera performances said "When you are surrounded by ugliness, beauty becomes something you cherish even more."

This is why we work so hard to be advocates for our orchestras, and all of our cultural institutions. We know we are not advocating for ourselves, but for the best of society and for all future generations. I'm sure when we were younger we believed that the world could evolve, and such conflicts would not devolve into unspeakable violence. I know I thought that education would improve and enlighten the world. But instead, we face more and more cuts in education funding, and a less educated world will only lead to more conflicts with violent outcomes; it takes thought and insight to find more creative solutions.

A disproportionate number of the cuts in education are found in music and arts programs. This shortsighted thinking will have a profound effect on the world should we not resist. After all, we know from multiple studies that music education leads to improved emotional outlook, enhanced social skills, greater mental health as we age, improved cognitive function, increased graduation rates, and greater skill in personal expression.

Of course there will always be terrible conflicts that appear unresolvable, and no one can eradicate violence from this world. But it seems to me that the best hope for future generations must come from education, and it appears too often that we live in a time when education is somehow viewed as "elitist". Conflicts will persist, but I don't see how it can get better with a less educated future, and music must be recognized as inherently valuable to achieving a more educated and enlightened society.

It is frightening to contemplate what might happen next in Donetsk, perhaps before this issue of *Senza Sordino* is published. Even as I write this afternoon, the media is reporting that a chemical plant in eastern Ukraine near Donetsk has been bombed and is burning out of control. A new ceasefire accord was reached on February 12, but it is the second such attempt, and we can only hope it succeeds in ending the violence. But music will always represent the best of humanity, and the defiance and resiliency of the human spirit. In a time of war the opera in Donetsk seems to me to be a revolutionary act of defiance, and I want to think of those artists as I perform with my colleagues, and as I travel as an advocate for musicians everywhere. Indeed, each one of us must see ourselves constantly as advocates for all musicians everywhere, and for the best of humanity. The 24-hour news channels might lead us to believe that the best of humanity is in short supply these days, but I don't believe that. I've seen and heard the best of humanity in every musician I've ever met, and I only wish it could be possible that I could be present at one of the operas in Donetsk.

Every note we play must stand as a statement against violence. When next we walk onto our stages, we should remember that across the world an opera company is producing music at the risk of their lives, insistent that the violence in their streets must not be allowed to diminish the value of life, nor the beauty that exists and remains possible to achieve.

As one of the performers in Donetsk expressed her hope: "You leave the house in the morning, and there's ice on the ground, wind in your face, snow falling, and the sound of bombs exploding everywhere. What can be better than to walk along and sing Strauss to yourself?"

(Note: many of the quotes in this report have been harvested from press accounts, most notably an excellent article by Shaun Walker in the Guardian, published on February 2, 2015, and viewable at http://www.theguardian.com/ music/2015/feb/02/donetsk-opera-ukraine-show-must-go-on)

Music Education and Hope

SENZA SORDINO
MAY 2015

A recent article posted on the Daily Beast website reported on how "Music Shields a Child's Psyche in a Time of War". The article describes a moment when Palestinian music students reach a road block assembled by Israeli soldiers, and in the midst of the tensions inherent in the conflict of the region, a student and a soldier each learn that the other can play the violin and they play for each other at the armed checkpoint.

Parts of the Daily Beast article probably could be viewed as controversial by some, as the conflicts in that part of the world have existed for centuries and we all have our deeply held views on world issues. But what is not controversial is that music has the power to unite even the most disparate of ideologies and soothe the deepest of conflicts, if only for a passing moment in the midst of profoundly ingrained conflict.

The posting also quoted from the collection of essays *Music, Music Therapy and Trauma: International Perspectives*, saying "Music, by raising the threshold for anxiety, can reduce the likelihood of resurgence of traumatic memories." Another quote was cited, saying that creativity can serve as a "fundamental part of healing...it is the refusal of victimhood and helplessness. Creating something new is an act of defiance in the face of destruction."

At a time when we are reminded of world conflicts through an unceasing din of 24-hour cable news channels, I am forever inspired and heartened by the fact that music continues to have the ability to unite people, and continues to be a force for change and strength for the people of all nations.

This month, to commemorate the centennial of an historical atrocity, one that has become known as the Armenian Genocide, 123 orchestral musicians from 43 nations gathered in the Armenian capital of Yerevan to perform a concert called Renaissance. Musicians of other genres also performed to remind the world of this event that must not be forgotten by future generations.

And in Baltimore, less than 48 hours after civil unrest spread through the city, the Baltimore Symphony performed a unifying outdoor free concert as a demonstration of peace in their city. Music Director Marin Alsop wrote: "With so much need alongside so much possibility, I hope we can use any opportunities we get to set an example and inspire others to join us in trying to change the world."

Music is a powerful tool for positive change in the world, and music education empowers creativity in all fields. The musicians of our orchestras must articulate this message tirelessly.

But music education is discouragingly underfunded in our own country. Robert Fitzpatrick, former dean at the Curtis Institute of Music, recently wrote that the past 50 years "have led to a decline in the quality of education in general, and an abandoning of the arts and arts education in particular."

Still, there are some signs of hope. I enjoyed a recent account of remarks made by Adam Savage of *Mythbusters* fame, who said "If you want the kids' test scores up, bring back band and bring back shop and get kids actually learning stuff instead of teaching them how to take a test." Our friends at Americans for the Arts recently posted an article titled "Arts Education Poised for Comeback in Nation's Largest School Districts." As more states adopt Common Core, they are implementing a program that mentions the arts approximately 75 times in its education standards. And, earlier this month, music was recognized as a core subject in draft federal education policy for the first time in history as part of the *Every Child Achieves Act of 2015*, which is designed to make adjustments to the policies of *No Child Left Behind*.

In New Orleans, a music education program called *Trumpets Not Guns* is providing musical instruments to students in communities that are at risk for falling prey to violence. A report from the Brady Campaign to End Gun Violence indicates that last year, handguns killed 10,728 people in America, as opposed to 58 in Israel, and 8 in Great Britain. Disproportionally at risk is the African American community. The *New York Times* recently wrote that "More than one out of every six black men who today should be between 25 and 54 years old have disappeared from daily life due to early deaths or incarceration."

Through innovative programs like *Trumpets Not Guns*, music education can inspire young people to reach for a higher ideal than the violence that too often surrounds them, proving that creativity is a positive act of defiance in the face of negativity. It is no exaggeration to say that music education saves lives.

If only I were naïve enough to believe it is that simple though. I have no delusions that we can eradicate violence from the world, and when I rise each morning I am aware that new accounts of human suffering will greet me should I turn on the television or read the paper. But I do believe that every concert we perform is an act of defiance in the face of destruction. Every note we play advocates peace. Every lesson we teach advocates knowledge. Every piece of music we learn and share advocates understanding.

We are the music makers and we are the dreamers of dreams. The musicians of our orchestras must lead this effort to change education, and change the world, just as musicians always have.

The life of a performing classical musician is difficult. It requires discipline, and an almost unnatural combination of confidence and self-criticism. It is easy for us to have moments of futility and apathy. After all, only fools never doubt. But the lives we have chosen to lead stand for unity and understanding in a fragile world. We must constantly renew our dedication, and we must constantly renew our hope.

As long as a single violin has the ability to unite Israelis and Palestinians, if only for a fleeting moment at a roadside blockade, I will remain hopeful for the world.

Darkness Audible

SENZA SORDINO
OCTOBER, 2015

From the first moment of my conscious memory, I have struggled with depression.

In the decade that I have spent traveling to meet with musicians, I have often seen a look in the eyes of those in the back of the room that I recognize all too well. Sometimes I understand that it is situational; after all I am often meeting with people fighting for the survival of their orchestras and their careers. And for musicians, it is often true that we see our very selves as inextricably linked with our careers.

A line from the 1998 movie *Hilary and Jackie*, about the great cellist Jacqueline du Pre, has always been haunting. As du Pre faces the effects of her progressive physical illness, she asks her husband "would you still love me if I couldn't play?" and the response is "If you couldn't play you wouldn't be you."

My strongest wish as ICSOM Chair has been to bring us all closer together, and to explore issues where we could better assist each other and grow together as musicians and humans. I have often said that musicians have a shared past, a shared present, and a shared future. I know that it is true that many of us share depression as well. I was compelled to finally write about depression by two events at the recent ICSOM Conference in Philadelphia.

A filmmaker and musician, John Beder, presented a short preview of a documentary project that he is working on called *Composed*, which chronicles how musicians deal with performance anxiety. In the film, I was impressed by the number of musicians willing to express their anxieties, seemingly without fear. When I was a younger musician, there was a stigma to talking about performance anxiety, and it struck me just how valuable this film, and these musicians' openness, will be to assist us all. Surely those who suffer from performance anxiety will be strengthened just knowing that they are not alone.

Also at the conference, in an effort to use our presence in the city as a symbol of community service, we held our first service event at an ICSOM Conference when we provided music and assistance at a soup kitchen in collaboration with Broad Street Ministry. On their Twitter feed, Broad Street Ministry wrote: "Today ICSOM extended radical hospitality by creating a trauma-informed space with music." Conference attendees served dinner to those in need, while others performed music.

While our musicians were playing as dinner was served, I looked into the eyes of those who had come to have a meal—in some cases I imagine perhaps the only real meal available to them in some time. The people were quite varied, some old, some young. They were in differing points of their distress, and some reacted joyfully to the music, and some merely ate their meals. But in the eyes of many I recognized the face of depression, and I realized that with a few bad turns none of us are too distant from the place where they find themselves.

A study of depression in various professions found that people working in the arts are the fifth most likely to suffer from depression. A more recent study found that 60% of musicians suffer from depression.

As ICSOM Chair, I have never faltered in my public message that we must hold on to hope, that music changes lives, that our mission as musicians should be to elevate a burdened world, and that our orchestras are indispensable vehicles for the enlightenment of the human spirit. I say those things both because they are true, and because I believe them. I also say those things because it has always been music that has allowed me to defeat depression on so many days.

Those of you who know me only in this public role might be surprised by this confession, but those closest to me surely are not. On most days I overcome it; in fact on almost every day I win the battle. I can find joy in music, and in performance. I am at my best when I am listening, either to people or music.

To those who might be reading this now through a veil of darkness, and to those of you whose eyes I have seen look forlornly into an uncertain future, I want you to know that you are not alone. What might feel like a singular secret to you is one that is shared by many, and empathy is nearer than you might think.

I also want to encourage those of you who are mercifully spared the descent of depression to find ways to be more supportive and sympathetic. There are those in your orchestras who find showing up every day to be a victory in itself over what can appear at times to be insurmountable obstacles. In our orchestras there can be an occasional "locker room mentality" where backstage rhetoric insults and isolates those who seem different or distant. This hurts our collective artistry. There is a meme that says "everyone you meet is fighting a battle you know nothing about." As musicians, artists, and especially as humans, we should remember that always.

I have often quoted Dylan Thomas, writing "Rage, rage against the dying of the light…" Those words serve as a mantra that leads me through darker days, and reminds me in moments of melancholia that I won't feel that way forever. I am empowered to resist the descent…and so are you.

In his book *Darkness Visible*, William Styron concludes by referencing Dante, writing:

"For those who have dwelt in depression's dark wood, and known its inexplicable agony, their return from the abyss is not unlike the ascent of the poet trudging upward and upward out of hell's black depths and at last emerging into what he saw as 'the shining world.' There, whoever has been restored to health has almost always been restored to the capacity for serenity and joy, and this may be indemnity enough for having endured the despair beyond despair."

In This Bleak Mid-Winter

SENZA SORDINO

DECEMBER, 2015

As I write at my desk tonight, it is four days before Thanksgiving in the United States. We are about to enter the holiday season, a season that in many ways is defined by music and memories. The musicians of ICSOM will be performing music that is all too familiar to us, with countless *Nutcrackers*, *Messiahs*, and holiday arrangements we have performed hundreds if not thousands of times. While we might find that music to be fatiguing, it will bring joy to many who listen, and they will find that joy at a time when it is greatly needed for the world.

Every holiday season is at least partly about the holidays that went before. Christmas carols and other holiday music are as evocative as the decades-old Super 8 millimeter films I have of me and my brothers opening presents, as our forever young parents watch wearily and happily.

My favorite carol has always been *In the Bleak Mid-Winter*, which I learned as a child from the Methodist hymnal, as a setting by Gustav Holst of a poem from the 1870s. But Benjamin Britten and other composers have also set the poem to music, and as a result there are many versions of this carol. Some are very religious, and others more secular. My favorite recording might be by the American singer-songwriter Shawn Colvin.

The bleakness of the carol's title merely describes the winter months, when "earth stood hard as iron, water like a stone" and "snow had fallen, snow on snow, in the bleak mid-winter, long, long ago."

This music is on my mind tonight, because as Thanksgiving approaches it is also ten days after the November 13 terrorist attacks in

Paris, and just a few days after the attacks in Mali. From the other room I can hear the non-stop drone of television news reporting that Belgium is under the highest alert for terrorist attacks, and pundits and candidates, alternately well-meaning and self-serving, debating and arguing over what we all should be doing to respond. The violent, disheartening events of the world in this mid-winter are indeed bleak.

Our esteemed editor, Peter de Boor, sent me a blog post he had found that discussed how the world should respond. The post urged us all:

> *If you make music keep making it. Make more of it.*
> *If you write, write more, publish more, speak more.*
> *If you make or watch film, or theatre, or dance, or comedy, or*
> *any other form of performance, it's now more important than*
> *ever.*
> *When our hearts are broken we have to keep our minds open.*

After these latest attacks on humanity, the world again turned to music and musicians responded.

Orchestras across the world dedicated their performances to the victims in France. The Metropolitan Opera performed the French national anthem *La Marseillaise*, as did the National Arts Centre Orchestra in Ottawa, along with so many others. Making it easier to do so, the listserve of the Major Orchestra Librarians Association (MOLA) sent out an immediate notice informing all their members how to access the score. And the Atlanta Symphony dedicated its performance of the Verdi *Requiem* to the victims in Paris.

The day after the attacks, a pianist arrived outside the Bataclan concert hall in Paris, the scene of so many deaths, and played John Lennon's *Imagine* for the gathered grieving crowd. As Brussels went on lock-down, a cellist appeared in front of armored vehicles to play Leonard Cohen's *Hallelujah*. To assist others in crisis, the Vienna Philharmonic launched a campaign to fund a house for asylum seekers that would give shelter to four families of refugees while providing language courses and music.

It is a troubled time for the world, but every generation has faced such a moment, and every generation has said "but this time it feels different." It is true that the attacks being perpetrated around the world, not just in European capitals but also in Beirut, Kenya, Nigeria, and in so many other places, represent a different type of assault on humanity and culture. These attacks are killing countless people, and they are also demolishing museums and artifacts, eradicating libraries, and destroying musical instruments.

Terrorism is designed to make us afraid, and designed to make us surrender our values in response. We must not accommodate the aims of terrorists. It is easy to see only the destructive people, but even while under assault there remains more kindness in this world than misanthropy. I remember an admonition from Mister Rogers I saw many years ago. When children would see television footage of such attacks, he would advise them to "look for the helpers. There are always people helping."

As humans and musicians, here is how we can best respond.

Seek out ways to show individual kindness to others, especially when it might not be seen or honored. This holiday season when many families are together there will be many people alone. Find ways to reach them. Volunteer to visit the elderly, who are all too often alone with memories of the past holidays. Volunteer to serve at a soup kitchen over the holidays. Give a coat to the homeless.

The musicians of our orchestras can join together to make donations of non-perishable goods to the food banks in our cities, or to raise money among ourselves for a donation to a needed cause in our cities.

This is how to respond to terrorism.

Further this year, when it is the tenth performance of the *Nutcracker* and we are exhausted with the repetition, look into the audience, mindful that they are arriving after seeing terrible carnage on TV. Make it our mission to demonstrate something beautiful to them at a time when they are wondering where beauty is to be found.

Share your thoughts and experiences with your orchestra's board members to make sure they understand their support for their orchestra is meaningful in their city, and meaningful in this world, perhaps now more than ever.

We will not be isolated, we will not be fearful, and we will not be apathetic.

When I was studying in Boston, my great teacher Lawrence Wolfe would write messages to me on my sheet music, which would frequently say "know no fear." As we move through this holiday season, and as we look for ways to respond to the world events, I urge us all to know no fear. We can respond with individual acts of kindness, we can respond by seeking out moments of joy and peace to share with everyone we meet, and our orchestras will respond as families, performing and welcoming the audiences who have arrived to share a moment of peace with us.

People of all religions and ideologies will be celebrating this month, and this year we must celebrate inclusiveness and acceptance together. While it can be easy to feel a sense of futility in the face of terrorism, musicians can join together inclusively and lead the way with our dedication and music, as music will always remain a force for good in our weary world.

> *What can I give you,*
> *Poor as I am?*
> *If I were a shepherd*
> *I would bring a lamb;*
> *If I were a wise man*
> *I would do my part;*
> *Yet what I can, I give you –*
> *I will give my heart.*
> *In the bleak mid-winter*
> *Long, long ago.*

The Age of Incivility

INTERNATIONAL MUSICIAN
FEBRUARY, 2016

Words matter, and facts matter, even if it might not seem that way in our current sociopolitical climate. Turn on the 24-hour news channels at any moment of the day, and you will be assaulted with a steady stream of harsh and insulting language, spewed by so-called experts who are inventing facts to fit into their own narrative.

It all seems so unnecessary. In recent days I have observed commentators on the news channels using incorrect historical references to make their points, misquoting historical figures, and using obscure references, while the interviewers don't seem to know to challenge them. It is as if the climate suggests that facts can be invented, and the loudest words are the only ones heard.

As musicians make the case for the importance of their orchestras and for support of the labor movement, our cause is best served when we offer an elevated message that inspires our supporters and our members. This is especially true for orchestras that exist in a philanthropic environment, dependent on a donor base to survive and thrive. The need for uplifting advocacy is crucial for the success of our organizations and our negotiations.

The musicians of our orchestras have led the way in this regard for decades, and have repeatedly fought diligently for the survival of their orchestras and the advancement of working conditions. Each orchestra that has taken on this cause of advocacy has informed all those that have followed. Every orchestra has learned and benefitted from the support of their colleagues through the International Conference of Symphony and Opera Musicians (ICSOM) and the AFM.

Orchestra musicians have found inspiring ways to make their case to their communities. Each holiday season, the musicians of the San Antonio Symphony engage in a caroling project at children's hospitals in their city. The musicians of the Utah Symphony created a program that brings music to the Huntsman Cancer Center. The Oregon Symphony Players Caroling Project brings music to numerous hospitals in their city, while the Baltimore Symphony Orchestra musicians serenaded patients and staff at Johns Hopkins Children's Center.

Chicago Symphony Orchestra violist Danny Lai recently wrote about his experiences traveling to the Middle East in 2013 bringing music to refugees, through his program called Music Heals Us. The Philadelphia Orchestra's principal trumpet, David Bilger, has been teaching one of the only trumpet students in Afghanistan through Internet lessons. Then he helped raise money for the student to study at Interlochen Center for the Arts through a GoFundMe campaign.

These are just a few examples of innovative advocacy. The musicians in orchestras everywhere are demonstrating the importance of investing in our orchestras and reaching all areas of the community. At the same time, they continue to perform great music in great concert halls as orchestras continue their revival from the depths of the 2008 economic downturn. Orchestras in Chicago, Cleveland, Pittsburgh, Indianapolis, Atlanta, and many others have seen increased attendance. Numerous large gifts have arrived, including a $25 million donation for the New York Philharmonic and a $1 million gift for the Buffalo Philharmonic Orchestra's endowment. And, in news just reported, we celebrate the long-awaited rebirth of the New York City Opera.

As of this writing, we hope for positive news from negotiations in Hartford, Grand Rapids, and Fort Worth. The musicians of those orchestras are making their case to the community in innovative and inspiring ways. Their friends and colleagues throughout ICSOM and the AFM stand ready to assist them, and all musicians everywhere, whenever needed.

It is clear that in this age of incivility, musicians can lead the way by continuing to offer an elevated message of hope to the world. In doing so, the world will surely benefit ... as will musicians everywhere.

Walls and Bridges

SENZA SORDINO
MARCH, 2016

As I reflect upon a decade of travel as ICSOM Chairman, it occurs to me it might be possible that I have visited more backstage orchestra lounges than all but a handful of negotiators. Often the personality of the musicians of the orchestra is represented in these lounges, and the musicians' history as well. I have seen old program books, posters, promotional buttons, and even materials from previous negotiations. There are bulletin boards with ICSOM settlements, newspaper clippings, letters from supporters, and commendations from mayors and governors that honor the musicians.

Some lounges have a wall of portraits, with pictures of former members of the orchestra that have retired or passed away. These portrait walls serve to provide the musicians who performed in the orchestra for so many years with a permanent presence in the orchestra's home. They are never forgotten, for they are always there.

I remember especially looking at the portraits of the former members of the Philadelphia Orchestra, backstage in the musicians' lounge in Verizon Hall at the Kimmel Center for the Performing Arts. I recognized many mentors and friends, too many of them now absent.

I've always liked that traditional toast "to absent friends", recited as a final glass is lifted in memory of departed friends and colleagues. I first learned it from a book by the great sportswriter Red Smith, in his collection of tributes to friends upon their passing.

The musicians' lounge also contains some portraits of people who played an important role in ICSOM's history. A picture of Irving Segall, who served as ICSOM Chair from 1974-1980, is there, along with Abe Torchinsky, for whom the ICSOM emeritus program is named.

Some walls in life are barriers, but these portrait walls in orchestra lounges are bridges. They honor the past as they strengthen the present, and they serve to ensure that those who have gone before will always be a part of the future.

Every orchestra undergoes a periodic generational shift, and that's as it should be. As is often said, time only moves in one direction. Youth invigorates our orchestras and preserves the art form. Every musician is connected in some way to a magnificent past, as they studied with a great teacher, who studied with a great teacher before, who studied with a great teacher before that. In its most generous interpretation, the passing of time means that every musician today has at least a passing link to Beethoven, Brahms, Stravinsky, and Bernstein, along with thousands of legendary orchestral musicians.

Openings in our orchestras provide opportunities to welcome a new generation to our ranks. But sometimes when a colleague retires it can seem as if they are too quickly absent from our lives, and our present is weakened if we don't remember, and celebrate, our past. It must be recognized by every new generation that there would be no orchestra for them to join if not for those who went before.

Some orchestras celebrate their former members perpetually. The Chicago Symphony Orchestra Alumni Association is very active, and the New York Philharmonic carefully maintains its archives, creating a website that provides countless hours of inspiration and education for the musicians who are performing in our orchestras today, as well as those who will join tomorrow.

Not every orchestra has a lounge backstage, as many perform in halls that are used by other performing organizations, or play in multiple halls to serve a wide community. But ways can still be found to celebrate former colleagues, and in doing so we will be forever connected to the achievements that preceded us. The opportunities for the next generation of musicians remain great, but as with all previous generations, those opportunities must be sought, protected and cultivated. The progress made thus far awaits new activism.

I have personally known all but three of the chairs of ICSOM. Sadly

I never had the opportunity to meet Irving Segall, as he passed away in 2004. But I have read a number of his letters, and studied his work. A website dedicated to his memory describes him in this way:

"Men who came to the bargaining table pounding fists, ready to plunge political knives into the backs of their opponents, were met by Irv's love for people and his compassionate nature—and they were calmed. They truly felt that they had been listened to and heard. He built bridges and lasting relationships – he made friends of everyone he met. Irv was devoted to justice. He had a very strong sense of what was 'the right thing to do.'"

In the musicians' lounge in Philadelphia, I spent a few moments looking at Mr. Segall's picture on the musicians' portrait wall. I was glad to see that a man so responsible for the growth of all our orchestras, and especially his own, is still a presence in the daily workplace of those who have succeeded him.

I hope more orchestras will create a portrait wall, or a place for pictures of those who have gone before. Every musician has earned a moment of honor from the current members of their orchestras, and everyone who has ever played in an ICSOM orchestra should always be thought of as a colleague. In this way we can honor our past, serve our present, and welcome our future.

Imagine a Better World

INTERNATIONAL MUSICIAN
JULY, 2016

This morning, I awoke to news of yet another violent attack, the deadliest mass shooting in America's history, this time in Orlando. While in these early hours we do not yet know the exact nature and causes of this horrific action, we do know that a man with an unspeakable weapon, unimaginable to the founding fathers, has killed at least 50 people and wounded many others.

I wasn't able to turn away from the coverage, even as the networks sought to fill airtime with pundits who could do nothing more than speculate. What did impress me was the thousands of people in Orlando lining up to give blood following the appeal of local hospitals. There are always more people wanting to help than there are people wanting to hurt.

It is too easy to turn away from these sad events. After all, our lives must continue. We have appointments to keep, work to do, yards to be mowed … at moments like this I am always reminded of W. H. Auden's "Musée de Beaux Arts":

> *About suffering they were never wrong,*
> *The Old Masters: how well they understood*
> *Its human position; how it takes place*
> *While someone else is eating or opening a window or just*
> *walking dully along …*

At this moment of collective pain, where sad events flood our lives through a din of media accounts, the world needs the statement of peace that musicians make with every note they play.

On June 13, the musicians of the Chicago Symphony Orchestra performed a benefit concert for the Greater Chicago Food Depository. They joined with other musicians of International Conference of Symphony and Opera Musicians (ICSOM) orchestras who have organized on their own to present concerts that demonstrate their desire to change the world, one note at a time. At this year's ICSOM Conference in Washington, DC, we will again perform music and offer service—this time at Central Union Mission, an organization that gives food, comfort, and shelter to the homeless in the District. This follows our Broad Street Ministry service at last year's conference in Philadelphia.

The musicians of the San Francisco Symphony performed a benefit for the SF-Marin Food Bank, North Carolina Symphony musicians organized a quartet performance to raise money for the victims of the 2015 earthquake in Nepal, and the musicians of the Dallas Symphony Orchestra performed a benefit for Dallas Court Appointed Special Advocates, an organization that assists abused and neglected children. In this past decade, the musicians of ICSOM have demonstrated astonishing generosity and goodwill towards each other, answering numerous ICSOM calls to action that have raised more than $1.5 million to assist colleagues in need during work stoppages or other difficulties. We have stood together as a united network of friends.

ICSOM is the most highly organized part of the AFM, with almost 99% of our members in the union. This is remarkable considering that 36% of our member orchestras are in "right to work" states. I believe we maintain this unity and build these friendships by offering our members ideals to work for, instead of only offering problems to work against. As we seek to serve our communities in even deeper ways, and stand together as messengers of peace in an all-too-often violent world, we also demonstrate the importance of our orchestras.

One of the major issues facing orchestras is the perception that our donor base is limited. We need to appeal to new donors by offering a message of hope and demonstrating how everyone benefits from great orchestras. We must believe that we can change the donor base, just as we must believe that we can change the world. In order to achieve anything you must first be able to imagine it.

Auden's poem continues:

> *In Breughel's Icarus, for instance: how everything turns away*
> *Quite leisurely from the disaster; the ploughman may*
> *Have heard the splash, the forsaken cry,*
> *But for him it was not an important failure; the sun shone*
> *As it had to on the white legs disappearing into the green*
> *Water, and the expensive delicate ship that must have seen*
> *Something amazing, a boy falling out of the sky,*
> *Had somewhere to get to and sailed calmly on.*

As artists, we must make efforts to change the world. We must not turn away and sail calmly on. As President Kennedy once said: "For while we cannot guarantee that we shall one day be first, we can guarantee that any failure to make this effort will make us last."

We are the music makers, and we are the dreamers of dreams. If we can imagine a better world, and demonstrate it through our music—through every lesson we teach, through every performance we play, whether in great concert halls or the halls of cancer hospitals—then we can continue to change lives by standing together for peace.

Hello, I Must Be Going

SENZA SORDINO
JUNE, 2016

Recently, I was in a used bookstore in Franklin, North Carolina, a tiny mountain town west of Asheville. On the plywood shelves I found a collection of ten disintegrating copies of *The Etude*, a current events classical music magazine, from 1947. Every page is fascinating, even though the magazines are so moldy they make your eyes water and your lungs ache. There are reports of Stravinsky working on his "new opera" (*The Rake's Progress*) and the American premiere of Mahler's Sixth Symphony by the New York Philharmonic. There is an article on music education by Erich Leinsdorf when he was music director of the Rochester Philharmonic, a notice of an invitation to the "young American conductor" Leonard Bernstein to conduct the Czech Philharmonic, and a brief news report on the acquittal of Berlin Philharmonic music director Wilhelm Furtwängler from accusations of Nazi activities. The editorial attitude of the magazine seems to suggest that the publishers saw it as topically progressive, even though the articles and advertisements contain many social stereotypes from the time. But inescapable in these post-war editions is the palpable sense that musicians represented a great hope for the new and uncertain world.

An opinion piece in the May, 1947, issue states, "The time has long since passed when musicians were expected to stand submissively, as 'souls apart' outside the gates of world progress, and not participate in the tremendous movements of the age…the participation of musically trained minds cannot fail to be of priceless value to the body politic at this startling moment in world history."

Nearly 70 years later, though the circumstances are different, the world again finds itself at a startling moment of unrest, and musicians most certainly will participate in the "tremendous movements" of this age as well.

When I step down from ICSOM this August, I will have served as Chair for ten years, a period longer than any of my predecessors. I will have also served on the Governing Board for twelve years and as an ICSOM delegate since 1993. I think that when anyone looks back on a moment of their life, it is unavoidable to wonder if they've made any difference in the grand scheme of things. I am certainly not immune from such self-questioning. But I do not have any doubts that the musicians of ICSOM have accomplished great things during this time, and I am very grateful that they have been so generous as to allow me to join with them in their efforts.

In this decade the musicians of our orchestras have endured numerous labor disputes, and outlasted a terrible recession. But they have not just endured, they have grown. They have stood against negativity, cultivated new techniques for negotiation and advocacy, and led the way in demonstrating how music is an inherent call for peace and inclusiveness.

The first major speech I gave to an ICSOM Conference was in San Diego in 2005, where as a new Member-at-Large to the Governing Board, I delivered a presentation called *A Message of Hope*. In those remarks I said, "Symphonic music will survive, and flourish, simply by proving its relevancy to the community."

In this decade the world has changed, as have I, as have we all. The world has seen violent acts met with violent rhetoric, and battles of equality are waged in statehouses and through social media. But throughout it all, in an ever more present way, musicians have stood for peace, and have taken action with their art to bring compassion to those who are hungry, alone, suffering and discriminated against. Humanity will always persevere in the face of violence, and music will forever be a response to hatred.

In an interview in 1972, Leonard Bernstein said, "The point is, art never stopped a war and never got anybody a job. That was never its function. Art cannot change events. But it can change people. It can affect people so that they are changed...because people are changed by art—enriched, ennobled, encouraged—they then act in a way that may affect the course of events…by the way they vote, the way they behave, the way they think."

If for a fleeting moment we could set aside the disagreements and maneuvering that infest all politics, from presidential politics to union politics, and reflect upon human relationships and the relationship of music to everything, the world could see that recent events have afforded us an opportunity for contemplation, if only voices of reason could be heard above the din.

In April, Noah Bendix-Balgley, concertmaster of the Berlin Philharmonic, stood on a stage in North Carolina where a controversial new law has imposed discrimination upon the LGBT community, and others. Following his performance of the Beethoven concerto, Bendix-Balgley (a native of Asheville) returned to the stage for an encore, not only carrying his violin but also a microphone. He spoke of his love for his home state and appealed for the realization that this law does not reflect who we are. He then performed the Adagio of Bach's Sonata No. 1 in G Minor in recognition of "all those who might not feel welcome or safe" due to the discriminatory law.

Wynton Marsalis once said "Sometimes excellence is a form of protest."

When I was elected ICSOM Chair at the 2006 Conference in Nashville, I knew we would have to overcome adversity. But it was our determined intention to offer our members ideals to work for, instead of merely angrily articulating things to work against. There have been difficult times, and many long nights. But overwhelmingly it has been an honor and a joy to serve as chair of ICSOM for this past decade. I have been inspired by every musician I have met, and I have enjoyed working with leaders in all roles of the field. Together, we have been able to articulate a positive message of hope while demonstrating how music unites all people and creates a more compassionate world.

In the future, I know that the musicians of ICSOM will continue to demonstrate that our concert halls are open to people of all religions and faiths, all races and nationalities, all sexual orientations and gender identities, and to people who respect music across the entire political spectrum.

The musicians of America's orchestras will continue to explore 21st Century methods to address 21st Century problems, and new styles of advocacy and activism for our orchestras and music will develop. Technology is a speedboat, but too often our organizations have been giant ocean liners, especially in the utilization of media. We cannot afford to move too slowly. Embracing new tools does not represent a surrender of tradition or solidarity, but rather it represents a crucial step in the preservation of our many institutions. As Mahler wrote, "tradition is not the worship of ashes, but the preservation of fire."

The musicians of ICSOM have made much progress. Orchestras across North America have supported each other through ICSOM Calls to Action, demonstrating that what happens to one orchestra happens to all of us. There is a bit less of the destructively negative rhetoric about the future of the arts that has, at times, dominated the press. By expressing our own views we have articulated a vision of what is possible to achieve in the future. Music is now a part of federal education policy, the economic impact of the arts for our cities is widely recognized, music therapy is increasingly being accepted as treatment for numerous medical conditions, and soon an opera singer, Marian Anderson, will be honored on United States currency.

I'd like to thank you all for your support and friendship over this past decade. As I have traveled in my role as ICSOM Chair it has been an honor to be welcomed in your concert halls, backstage lounges, and homes. Musicians have accomplished great things by uniting together, but there is much work left to be done. I am confident that the next generation of ICSOM leadership will take the organization to its greatest heights, and tremendous success awaits the next Chairperson.

As I look to my own future, I do not yet know the next steps on my path, or where the road ahead might lead. But I do know, like Frost, that I have promises to keep, and miles to go before I sleep.

My love to you all,

Bruce

Selected speeches

2006-2016

Address to the 2006 Conference of the Organization of Canadian Symphony Musicians

WINNIPEG, MANITOBA
AUGUST 4, 2006

As the *New York Times* proclaimed earlier this year, this should be recognized as the golden age of classical music. But instead, far too often, we face negative messages, and these messages are frequently placed by our own managements. We constantly hear of structural deficits, and of sustainability in the community. Ours is the only industry I can think of where some managements seek to both promote and undermine the product at the same time.

But, we have the convenience of the truth on our side. And the truth is that orchestras are invaluable to their communities. An orchestra is indispensable to a city, for the people who live there, the children who learn there, and the companies that do business there.

Since the Players' Conferences came into being, salaries have gone up dramatically. The number of full time orchestras has increased, and benefits that add to the livelihood of the performing artist have improved. While we acknowledge these facts at times, here is what we all too often fail to say: None of these improvements would have occurred on their own, and none of them would have occurred without OCSM, ROPA, ICSOM and our union. Few managements have ever offered to increase salaries and benefits merely because it was the right thing to do. They did so only when they were compelled to by a unified body of musicians. This is a unity that has become international.

Now we stand at a moment of incredible opportunity for orchestras. For too long the messages in our seasons' glossy brochures have conflicted with the messages in our inky newspapers. I would suggest to you that musicians have been losing the PR war, and we must proclaim now that we will no longer cede that victory.

Study upon study has shown the positive economic impact that the arts have on a city, and demonstrated that giving to the arts is not just giving a gift, it is making a tangible investment in your community. But still, some managers bemoan the sustainability of growth. Where it is asked "how can our community continue to support the arts" the answer must be, resoundingly, "How can we afford not to?"

This will be the focus of ICSOM over these next few years. We will work to spread the message far and wide that orchestras are not only educationally rich, they are economically sound. Our orchestras promote business and the name of our great communities. In these matters it must be acknowledged that for a community's cultural, educational and economic life, where the arts are concerned…the greater the investment, the greater the return.

We must work to make this truth more apparent, and for that…the responsibility falls on our shoulders. We must rededicate ourselves to our communities, investing in them just as we ask them to invest in us. The average tenure of an executive director in our industry is just 5 years. For musicians and the Board, it is much longer. *We* form the community and the family that surrounds an orchestra. If we work to improve communication with our boards, then a new executive director and music director will have to adapt to that spirit of community in order to succeed. We must reach out to our Boards in new and innovative ways. And also…we need to reach out to each other.

The communication between all of the Players' Conferences has always been strong, but we can work to strengthen it even further. The stronger the communication, the stronger we all are. We must reach out to strengthen our ties to our locals as well. We must always work together toward a healthy and positive debate on the issues before us, and we must always remember that we need not concern ourselves with attacks on our orchestras from our managements if we are at all willing to attack ourselves from within.

While I am filled with hope for all that we can accomplish, I am also not without reason. Many of our colleagues face difficulties. We must send the message that we will always stand together.

The negative rhetoric about our industry must change, and we are the ones to change it and mold it into a positive message that we can spread to our constituencies and their communities. Our orchestras can serve as beacons of hope and symbols of excellence in a world that is too often without hope and too often content with mediocrity. The true nature of anything is what it becomes at its highest. In this way we can inspire our communities and lead them to a higher level.

This we did with our lives for a reason. While it is (and has always been) so in vogue for orchestral musicians to be cynical, it is not beyond us to continue to indulge in our dreams. The greatest musicians among us are those who are still inspired by the opportunity to inspire. Through uniting together and reaching out to our communities, we can and will insure that the arts continue to thrive, and we will enrich the lives of our audiences while inspiring the next generation of musicians.

Address to the First International Orchestra Conference of the Federation International des Musiciens

APRIL 8, 2008
BERLIN, GERMANY

I'd like to begin by telling you just a little about the organization I represent, the International Conference of Symphony and Opera Musicians, or ICSOM. Our members are 4000 musicians in the 51 largest orchestras in the United States. If the "international" part of our name seems a misnomer, it is because when we were founded we were indeed international, having orchestras from Canada in our membership. But, in 1975, the Canadian Orchestras formed their own conference, and they are represented here in Berlin by my dear friend, Francine Schutzman.

ICSOM represents some of the most well-known orchestras in the world, such as the Philadelphia Orchestra and the Chicago Symphony. But we also represent smaller orchestras that are some of the finest artistic institutions found anywhere, such as the San Antonio Symphony and the Oregon Symphony. While some of our orchestras are not international names, they are intrinsically linked with their cities, and they serve their communities through the highest level of public service. I am a member of the North Carolina Symphony, an orchestra that performs free concerts for over 55,000 school children every year. In my role as ICSOM chairperson, I have traveled over 60,000 miles to hear our musicians perform, from Puerto Rico to Honolulu. It is indeed a great pleasure to be able to add to my travels this great gathering of musicians in Berlin, and it is an honor to be asked to speak with you today.

The topic I was asked to address is "What can be done so people don't undervalue or overvalue musicians?" I must say that, unfortunately, in the United States we need not concern ourselves with the issue of musicians being 'over'valued. The orchestras of America face a seemingly endless onslaught of negative prognostications, and for many musicians the struggle to spread a positive message of hope to our communities is as vital as the daily regimen we undertake to maintain our craft.

While there are many orchestras that are thriving, in other places we must be our own advocates. We face governments that seek to balance their budgets by slashing arts funding, despite the fact that every dollar invested in the arts returns seven dollars in revenue. The non-profit culture industry in the United States generates over $166 billion every year, and provides 5.7 million jobs. Together we work to counteract a negative perception of the future of classical music.

Recently, one of our member orchestras, the Jacksonville Symphony, faced an egregious lockout by their management in a plan to reduce the size of that excellent orchestra into something that their board felt was "more manageable". This position was taken by people who are supposedly stewards of the community in a city that has seen a 35% expansion of the economy in the past five years.

I am delighted to tell you that the lockout was not successful, and that the musicians are now back on stage. This was largely due to an unprecedented show of support by the musicians of North America who responded to a Call to Action issued from ICSOM by donating nearly $100,000 to support the musicians. The support of the unified musicians across the continent made the lockout a national issue, and demonstrated that the positive message of the musicians within their community can overcome a negative message perpetrated by an underperforming management.

No sooner had the issue been resolved in Jacksonville then another crisis appeared, this time for the Columbus Symphony in the state of Ohio. There, the board and management proposed to resolve financial difficulties by eliminating 22 musicians.

The climate that leads to these incidents is one of historic record. For many years, a pervasive sense of doom has lingered over the orchestral industry in America, at times promulgated by the industry itself. When I first joined the Virginia Symphony in 1979, I was told that the audience for classical music would soon be dead. But now, nearly 30 years later, I see the same audiences I saw then. The negative pronouncements ignore the fact that in America we are seeing a rise in attendance, a rise in classical music downloads, and a proliferation of beautiful new concert halls. The artistic level of our orchestras, with budgets both large and small, has never been higher.

The venerable *Wall Street Journal* recently proclaimed "Contrary to the rumors, symphony orchestras have a bright future."

But, why do these rumors persist at all? I have a newspaper article that asserts "25 Symphonies Doomed to Die." Disturbing news, to say the least. Until, that is, you realize that the article was published in 1970, and that all of the orchestras exist to this day. In fact, many have risen to illustrious heights.

One of our success stories is the Nashville Symphony, an orchestra that declared bankruptcy just 20 years ago. Today this orchestra is a model of excellence recognized throughout the world. The orchestra has just opened its new concert hall which is acknowledged by all as one of the finest on any continent. The community rose to save this orchestra. And now, the symphony has revitalized the historic downtown of Nashville, and brought international attention to the city through its award winning recordings.

There are many successes to celebrate. The Fort Worth Symphony is receiving rave reviews for a Carnegie Hall appearance, the Florida Orchestra is announcing gifts totaling over $3 million, the Buffalo Philharmonic is aggressively building its endowment, the Oregon Symphony has seen a 20% increase in attendance, and the New York Philharmonic is receiving more press coverage than the Oscars following its tour to North Korea. And yet, we still hear the incessant drum beat that professes that the arts are not sustainable in certain cities.

It seems to me that the arts are the only business that seeks to resolve financial difficulties by offering an inferior product to its public. Ballet companies turn to recorded music, and symphony boards propose a drastic reduction in the size of the orchestra. It is clearly a misguided approach.

I think it is less a question of whether musicians are overvalued or undervalued, but rather, how do we work to ensure that they are indeed valued? There are many ways to reach out to our communities and build the sense of family that should surround every orchestra in its city.

"Community" is a buzz word in the orchestra world today. We must strive to make sure that "community" refers not only to an investment in us, but that it also means that musicians invest in our community. To establish indelibly the positive sense of community that our musicians seek to develop, musicians must learn to break the fourth wall.

In theater, the fourth wall is the imaginary wall between the stage and the audience, the other three walls being formed by the shell of the stage. The term has been adapted from the theater to include books, film, and television.

Musicians in symphony orchestras can adapt the term to serve a new purpose as well. All too often in our concert halls there seems to be a dividing line between the orchestra and the audience. To establish a closer relationship with our audiences, boards, and community leaders, orchestra musicians need to break that fourth wall. This would mean establishing a connection with the audience and inviting them into the community that surrounds every orchestra. And further, it would mean expanding that community to all constituents of our cities.

At a time of uncertainty in the world, where discord seems more valued than debate, where doctrines of fear and rhetoric of violence replace the inspirational words of hope that have, at moments of past crisis, led the citizens of the world to aspire to something greater than themselves, art (as Bernard Holland wrote)...art is our fragile claim to control over our lives.

Everywhere we look there is evidence of the power of symphonic music. It is seen and heard through historical events. It was experienced internationally when Leonard Bernstein conducted Beethoven's Ninth Symphony here in this great city at the fallen Berlin Wall. It is heard on one of my favorite vinyl records; an amazing live recording by the Boston Symphony of Mozart's Requiem at a memorial mass for President Kennedy in January of 1964. I felt it on the lawn at Duke University immediately following the terrorist attacks of September 11, where thousands of people held candles as they listened reverently to their own symphony orchestra, a scene repeated throughout the world by hundreds of orchestras in hundreds of locations. It is felt in the response of our audiences and seen throughout our communities as we help attract businesses, educate our children, and spread the name of our great cities.

We must remember, this we did with our lives for a reason. While it is and has always been so in vogue for orchestral musicians to be cynical, it is not beyond us to continue to indulge in our dreams. The greatest musicians among us are those who are still inspired by the opportunity to inspire. Through uniting together and reaching out to our communities, we can and will ensure that the arts continue to thrive, and we will continue to enrich the lives of our audiences as we improve the livelihood of our colleagues, all while inspiring the next generation of musicians.

Wherever an orchestra is in trouble, let us all respond. Wherever a musician is in need, let us all respond. Wherever a negative image of the arts is produced, let us answer with a positive message of hope. Let our community of musicians serve as an example to those places across the globe that are aching to hear a positive message.

It is a right of the people that they not be deprived of hope. As they hear our music, let them also hear our voices.

While many of the issues that surround orchestras are indeed local issues, there is no doubting the power in collective good will. Let those of us in this room resolve to build an international network of support. Let us establish contacts and friendships that will allow us to shine an international spotlight that will serve as a beacon for the arts in every community across the world. We are the advocates for our art form, we are the advocates for our communities, and we are the advocates for our children. Through our music, we offer a message of hope that the world is longing to hear.

Testimony before the United States Congress House Committee on Education and Labor

HEARING ON THE ECONOMIC AND EMPLOYMENT IMPACT OF THE ARTS AND MUSIC INDUSTRY
MARCH 26, 2009
WASHINGTON, DC

Good morning, Chairman Miller, Ranking Member McKeon and members of the Committee. My name is Bruce Ridge. I am Chairman of the International Conference of Symphony and Opera Musicians, or ICSOM, which is a conference of the American Federation of Musicians. I'm also a double-bassist in the North Carolina Symphony. On behalf of ICSOM's thousands of members and AFM's tens of thousands of members – comprising over 230 affiliated locals across the country, including Local 367 in Vallejo and Local 424 in Richmond, in your district, Mr. Chairman – I thank you for your attention to this issue.

In 1932, my orchestra was founded by the Works Progress Administration. That was also a time of economic crisis, but instead of cutting back, we invested in the arts.

Critics sometimes say that classical music is just for the elite. But as an orchestral musician, I know how much everyone loves to hear us play. The numbers bear this out: Opera attendance has increased 40% since 1990. Classical music accounts for 12% of sales on I-Tunes, and music schools across the country are seeing an all-time high in numbers of applicants.

Musicians don't do it for the money. We're ultimately the nation's biggest donors to the arts, and we're the ones who sacrifice to keep orchestras alive in hard times. We happily give to the arts, but we must still pay doctors' bills, make rent, and feed our families.

I've been fortunate in my career. I started playing at age 10, and I've worked steadily as an orchestral musician for 30 years. By age 15, I was a working professional in the Virginia Symphony. I would go from school to symphony, then play in late-night jazz clubs I was too young to legally get into otherwise. Back home by 3 am, I'd be sitting in school just a few hours later. Although I may have started a bit younger than others, my story is not atypical. Many classical musicians work several jobs, driving from town to town as members of a "Freeway Philharmonic." Some members work in as many as four different orchestras – each a different two hour commute from home, and each with its own set of concerts, rehearsals, and community involvement.

In today's economic climate, the challenges for working musicians are growing ever more serious. Many orchestras face the prospect of reduced seasons, layoffs, lower wages, and higher health care premiums. This is a national problem. The musicians of the Cincinnati Symphony, one of the world's finest orchestras, recently accepted an 11% pay cut. The Baltimore Opera Company has filed for bankruptcy. The Santa Clarita Symphony, in your district Congressman McKeon, cancelled its 2009 season. The musicians of the Honolulu Symphony are now seven weeks behind in paychecks. On a daily basis my phone rings with more news of yet another orchestra's financial crisis.

For musicians, the losses are immeasurable. Some must sell their instruments to make ends meet, while others face the loss of their careers altogether. Many of these musicians have children or spouses who depend on them and who also suffer from these cutbacks. How could I respond, when a woodwind musician asked me how she could afford to take her child to the doctor after her orchestra's proposed cutbacks?

Our losses are everyone's losses. If musicians can't afford to stay in the profession, the nation will lose its music.

Musicians are small business people, patching together royalties, concert fees, and union benefits like session fees, pension, and health care to come up with a decent living. On Broadway, musicians face replacement by recorded music substituted for live music. In Hollywood, outsourcing film scores to musicians abroad threatens the livelihood of American musicians.

Congress can make – and indeed already has made – a big difference in these musicians' lives. The American Jobs Creation Act helped our recording musicians by providing tax incentives for domestic film production. Pension reform legislation has also helped the AFM keep its pension plan available to musicians. Chairman Miller, we thank you for your leadership on this important issue.

Several members of this Committee have co-sponsored H.R. 848, the Performance Rights Act, which gives recording artists a right to royalties when their performances are played over AM-FM radio. Recorded music makes money for radio, but radio doesn't pay performers a single cent. The Performance Rights Act would correct this inequity, and we ask you to consider supporting this important legislation.

Entertainment is America's second-largest export, and music is essential to nearly all of its forms, either standing alone or as part of theater, film, and television. We can count the dollars, but we can't count the value of music to the American spirit. We saw it when the New York Philharmonic traveled to North Korea on a mission of diplomacy and artistry. The nation and the world were electrified by those images. And we see it here at home when my WPA-founded North Carolina Symphony plays free concerts for tens of thousands of schoolchildren each year. I can't even go to the grocery store without people telling me how much it meant to them when the North Carolina Symphony played at their school. The value of these experiences cannot be measured, and must not be lost.

On behalf of musicians everywhere, I thank you for this opportunity to address the Committee.

Keynote Address

UNIVERSITY OF MICHIGAN'S AMERICAN
ORCHESTRA SUMMIT II
MARCH 22, 2012

It is a great pleasure to be with you this afternoon at the University of Michigan. This is my first visit to Ann Arbor, and I'm finding that the many Michigan graduates in ICSOM orchestras across America were right when they told me that I would love this beautiful town and campus. I'd like to thank Mark Clague and the University of Michigan for inviting me to speak, and for giving me this opportunity to share my views on the current state of orchestras in America. Two of my closest colleagues on the ICSOM Governing Board are graduates of the school of music here at Michigan, and they encouraged me to begin my remarks by saying "Go Blue!" Of course, I'm happy to say that on their behalf, but as a Tar Heel, I hope you'll forgive me when I say that I do tend to think of a slightly different shade of blue.

The International Conference of Symphony and Opera Musicians, or ICSOM as we are known, was founded fifty years ago this year in meetings at Roosevelt University in Chicago. This summer, representatives of the nation's top 51 orchestras, along with our many friends, will gather once again in Chicago to celebrate the great advances of symphonic music in North America over these past fifty years.

ICSOM was founded by a group of extraordinary and fearless musicians who came together in a most remarkable way, defying the threat of retribution from their managements, the threat of persecution from their union, and even the scrutiny of the federal government to make labor history. The founding musicians of ICSOM first came together in the sixties, a time of great change for all of America. Those musicians bravely won recognition from their union, and played instrumental roles in the creation of the National Endowment for the Arts, as well as elevating the profile of the symphonic musician in America. They were advocates for the future, and that advocacy is as strong today as it was at the moment of the organization's birth.

The need for ICSOM was great at the moment of its founding. Symphonic musicians, despite their artistic renown, were treated terribly...both by their managements and their union. A famous quote from around that time came from Dr. Wilfred Bain, the dean of the Indiana University School of Music, who said:

> "Snaring top flight musicians is easy, because people who push brooms are treated better than symphony players."

ICSOM's publication, *Senza Sordino*, reported that in the 1960's:

> "...most musicians in major symphony orchestras were employed little more than six months annually, at a yearly salary that was barely a living wage....Musicians had little job security and were subject to immediate and arbitrary dismissal."

It was a time where the field either had to move forward, or dissolve into irrelevancy. Through the leadership of America's musicians and with the work of ICSOM, the field did indeed move forward. Orchestral musicians were able to build a successful artistic life, with job security, with the freedom to take artistic chances, and with benefits that would allow them to care for their own children even as they dedicated their lives to advancing the education of the children of their communities, and to elevating the profiles of their cities through their diligent service.

On October 26, 1963, John F. Kennedy said:

> "I see little of more importance to the future of our country and our civilization than full recognition of the place of the artist. I look forward to an America which will

reward achievement in the arts as we reward achievement in business or statecraft. I look forward to an
America which will steadily raise the standards of artistic
accomplishment and which will steadily enlarge cultural
opportunities for all of our citizens."

Despite the great advances made, President Kennedy's aspiration for
the artists of America has yet to be fulfilled. Fifty years later, musicians
again find themselves at a crossroad, and the call for advocacy and activism is sounded once again.

There is a negative view of the future of the arts in America that is
prevalent and persistent. This is especially true for orchestras, but the
musicians of America's orchestras do not accept this view. We recognize,
however, perhaps more acutely than some, that in a time where the media
culture dictates that image is everything, symphony orchestras have a
serious image problem. This image problem inhibits fundraising, govern-
mental support, audience building, and the expansion of the donor base.

Also perhaps more acutely than some, the musicians of America's
orchestras realize that the field is largely doing this to itself.

Other fields, with far less to offer, have mastered the art of messaging.
The "truth" they sell is in their message; but even if you have an effective
truth, it will not be heard unless you also have an effective message. On
a national basis, our field does not have such a message.

What is the truth about the arts and music in America?

The non-profit arts and culture industry accounts for $166 billion in eco-
nomic activity every year, and supplies 5.7 million jobs. In Michigan alone,
the arts employ more people than the plastics industry and account for 6.5%
of the economy. On a national average, every dollar that government invests
in the arts returns seven dollars to the community, and locally that figure
is much higher. Classical music accounts for 12% of downloads on ITunes,
and in the Commonwealth of Massachusetts, the Boston Symphony alone
accounts for over $166 million in economic activity every year.

But these are not the words of advocacy that emanate from within the
field. Instead, the symphonic "industry" in America generates programs
that state:

"Red Alert!"

"American Orchestras: Endangered Species?"

"The Perilous Life of Symphony Orchestras"

When I see these quotes, I certainly don't want to donate to orchestras. I might not even want to attend. Why should people leave their homes, drive downtown, find parking, spend money on dinner out, all to hear a concert by an organization whose own managerial leadership says that fewer and fewer people are attending. In the face of these self-fulfilling prophecies, it might be true that donations and attendance are down in some places, but have we ever stopped to ask ourselves why? I suggest we haven't, and I further suggest that if organizations like the League of American Orchestras want us to start telling the quote *Brutal Truth*, well, then we should tell it.

I named this address *Danger Will Robinson! How Hyperbolic Negative Rhetoric is Hurting America's Orchestras*. I realize that the reference is dated and might be lost on some younger attendees to this summit. But a long time ago, longer ago than even I can remember, there was a television show called *Lost in Space,* with an alarmist robot which would flail its robot arms at the mere suspicion of danger, alerting young Master Robinson with the phrase *"Danger Will Robinson!"* It became a bit of a pop culture catch phrase, and I've used it here because I didn't want to be left out of the exaggerated, alarmist rhetoric.

The good news to be told about the field's negativity is that all of this destructiveness is nothing new. As mind-boggling as it seems, the field seems to have been dedicated to promoting its inevitable demise for quite some time now. Every few years a new report comes out that suggests that orchestras are not sustainable and that a new model must be discovered. It is always called something slightly different, such as *"The New Paradigm"* or *"The New Economic Reality"*, or simply *"The New Model"* but it is always the same. I've taken to calling it *"The New Apocalypticism."*

We can trace this phenomenon back quite a long way.

An article from United Press International was titled *25 Orchestras Doomed to Die*, and it forecast the demise of 25 symphony orchestras throughout America. It specifically set the death of the Atlanta and Houston Symphonies for the early part of the decade, while Baltimore and Dallas would survive until the middle of the decade, and Seattle might make it 8 years.

All of this is terrifying, except this article was published in 1970, and the predictions have been proven wrong for forty years.

It went on to say (*remember, in 1970*) that "orchestras have one alternative to going out of business." They must "reshape—either by reducing the size of orchestras from 100 to 90 musicians or by shortening seasons."

Does any of this sound familiar?

An article from June of 1969, published in *Time Magazine*, quoted "an expert in orchestral finances" as saying "Between 1971 and 1973, we stand a very good chance of losing at least one-third, if not half of our major symphony orchestras."

We have a document written by the president of the board of the Chicago Symphony, who said:

> "The (Chicago Symphony) now must solve a problem which has arisen from economic conditions beyond its control. A deficit has been incurred, and undoubtedly there will be annual deficits for some years to come. This affects the future of the orchestra."

And he continued:

> "Our problem does not differ in kind from the financial problem that faces each of the major orchestras in the United States."

This is especially alarming, isn't it?... that an orchestra as great as the Chicago Symphony could face this predicament. I would be more concerned had this not been written on April 1, 1940.

There is one great sentence in this 1940 document though. In a message that all managers should heed, especially today, the board chair states:

> "We cannot reduce our expenses below our present level without seriously endangering our standard of symphony music, which would soon result in endangering our principal source of income."

The negative rhetoric about the unsustainability of orchestral music permeates the culture even more prominently today, as the internet provides unedited forums for those who profess that they are worried about an explosion, even as they spend a lot of time lighting fuses. How long are we going to listen to this pablum without calling shenanigans?

Critics of what I am saying might suggest that I am naïve, and that I am not acknowledging that we are, in fact, living in different times. Please allow me to assuage you of that concern. We *are* living in different times. We cannot continue as we have been. We must change.

We must stop doing this to ourselves.

We live in a media age, at a time when the culture moves quickly. The successful businesses are the ones that can adapt to new ways of messaging, and control their image. People want to respond to positive messages. People will donate to, and invest in, organizations that inspire them, and they will not invest in organizations that question their own sustainability. The current message of our field, on a national level, simply put, is a poor fund-raising and marketing message.

Technology is a speed boat, and our field is a giant ocean liner. It takes forever to get turned around. We are behind the times in the utilization of free media, in social networking, in innovative marketing, in lobbying, and in advocacy.

I sometimes doubt that our field really understands new media. I once heard a prominent manager give an explanation of Reality TV, which he described as "meeting a demand from the public for that type of programming." But there was no demand for reality TV...it was a *manufactured* demand. A few executives decided that it would be great to work in television if it wasn't for all those actors and writers, and inspired by the success of *Survivor*, they realized that drivel could be produced for next to nothing. Upon that realization, they set upon a marketing campaign to convince the American public that this was indeed the programming they wanted. Reality TV is a marketing ploy. The broadcast industry understands how to sell rubbish, but far too often we don't understand how to sell masterpieces.

I'd like to stress that I am making these statements about our field on a national level. Locally, many of our orchestras are articulating a positive message, led by excellent managers, and they are seeing tremendous success. These successes are all the more remarkable in light of the economic downturn of 2008. The story to be told is not that orchestras are struggling, but rather that so many are doing well. The performance of most of our orchestras during this time is a testament to the viability of what we do, not evidence of the need for radical change. But, as a field, on a national level, we tend to study our failures to create so-called new models. What other business does this? Who patterns their future on their failures, while ignoring their successes?

Let's look at a few recent success stories...stories that probably won't get much attention from our national organizations:

Recent headlines have stated:

"Colorado Symphony (cue drumroll) is back in the black"

"...the Hawai'i Symphony Orchestra will make its long-awaited debut March 4, marking the return of a professional orchestra to the state more than two years after the Honolulu Symphony played its final note."

"...another milestone in the Alabama Symphony's rise."

"Buffalo Philharmonic shows surplus under economic challenges"

"St. Louis Symphony ticket sales, gifts, endowment grow in 2011"

"How Classical Music Is Changing Young Lives"

"Grammy win for Nashville Symphony ...signal(s) Nashville's "golden age of classical music"

I'm reminded that it was just a few short years ago that the *New York Times* proclaimed that "This is the Golden Age" for classical music, going on to say that "Rumors of classical music's demise haven't just been exaggerated, they've been dead wrong."

Such positive press should have been universally promoted by all aspects of the field, but instead, the *Times* article was met with derision by some managers, as if somehow the positive account didn't fit into their plans.

Where else can we find positive news to promote together as an industry...news that could inspire our donors and educate our supporters?

Well, the San Francisco Opera's recent production of Wagner's *Ring Cycle* sold at a rate of 99.9% per performance, generating over $7.2 million at the box office. The New York Philharmonic surpassed its fund raising goal by nearly half. The North Carolina Symphony met a goal for a matching grant of $8 million. The Kansas City Symphony has just opened its spectacular new concert hall which will be an iconic image for the city.

The Metropolitan Opera is seen in over 1500 movie theaters in 45 countries while performing to sold-out houses. In other artistic genres, last year the Metropolitan Museum of Art saw an attendance of 5.7 million, its highest attendance in 40 years! In 2010, in the depths of the worldwide economic downturn, arts giving grew by 5.7%, reaching $13.3 billion.

Still, despite this positive news, there is no musician in America that fails to recognize the need for analysis of our field, and the need for change. All things change in time. But, how can our field fail to recognize that destructive rhetoric is the enemy of change? Musicians cannot partner with those who spread a damaging message.

There can be no authentic conversation about change in our field that excludes executive compensation and artist management fees.

Privately, almost every manager I've ever spoken with has expressed concern over the escalation of guest artist fees and the power of the artists' management agencies. But they can't say it publically, as they rely on their services. The League of American Orchestras can't bring that into their "Red Alerts" or "Brutal Truths", because they receive advertising revenue from those agencies.

It is well-known that there is tension between many musicians and the League of American Orchestras, so let's talk about it. I actually have a slightly different viewpoint. I think the field needs the League, but we also need the League to change. We need the League to use its resources in developing positive messaging. There is a seemingly instinctive negativity that comes from the League at times, and it is being noticed by some of its own members. The League relies on the collection of $1.9 million in dues money to survive, and to pay considerable salaries to its upper staff. This year, one ICSOM orchestra left the League, citing the "dispiriting" rhetoric that emanates from the League. There are other managers who have privately expressed this same thought. I feel that the League must address its image problem, for if it was to fail, imagine the negative press then. The media instinctively covers the negative story, and if the League fails it would be perceived as a death knell for all symphonic music. It wouldn't be, of course but it would be perceived that way.

I have done a lot of work for the League though, certainly as much as any other sitting ICSOM Chair. I have spoken at League conferences, served on the faculty for many training sessions, and I've met regularly with the leadership. This year, I will again attend the League conference, even though I have expressed my concern to the leadership of the League that their programming may be viewed as negative by musicians, and that the chasm may well widen.

Many wonderful people work at the League, but the League must become an organization that more effectively uses its resources for advocacy.

I recognize the difficulty inherent in that though….I really do. For example, when a board member of the League makes very public and damaging statements, particularly in a published editorial about how a specific orchestra is unsustainable, terrible harm is done to the field, to that orchestra, to that community, and to relationships throughout all areas of the industry. The leadership of the League must speak out against such destructiveness, and when they do not it weakens the organization in the eyes of musicians and managers alike.

I understand the difficulty of such decisions, and such statements. As ICSOM Chair, I once had to make a very difficult decision about a legendary figure who found himself in a situation that was not acceptable to the ICSOM Governing Board. It was heartbreaking, as this legendary person did more to elevate the lives of symphonic musicians that any other person in the past 50 years. It was a devastating personal decision for me, so powerful that it seriously damaged my health for a two year period. I understand how hard it is to make the difficult decisions, and to issue the controversial statements. But that is what leadership is all about. And if the League wants to be a leader in our field, it can no longer stand by in silence and then claim to not understand why musicians and managers alike find the organization "dispiriting."

Musicians have willingly entered the room for a partnership, only to find themselves a little singed in the process. I think the whole field had hope for the Collaborative Data Project, which brought ICSOM, ROPA and the AFM into an effort to work with the League to develop a shared data set, as it has long been recognized that the numbers collected by the field for analysis are inconsistent at best. But instead, the numbers we were studying were given to a researcher who has produced damaging documentation based on imprecise data that has been used against musicians. This type of action is not positive, and this is not collaboration.

It brings me no pleasure to issue criticism of anyone, but our field is facing challenges and we must stop doing this to ourselves. In fact, in my writings I have called on musicians to avoid casting aspersions towards the League, and I have asked the League to issue similar statements to its members about the way they regard their musicians. While I've yet to hear my public appeal matched, I remain hopeful.

Still, I would much rather talk about solutions, and I will, but we can't identify the solutions without first identifying the problems.

Right now, at this very moment, there are orchestra managements preparing their organizations for extended and unnecessary work stoppages. One in particular will be prominently in the press as early as this fall, but I don't want to name the organization as I have hope that the management will avoid this destructive path. There is still time. But resources spent in this direction are also resources that could be spent promoting their organization.

Think of the damage done to the image of orchestras in the mind of an American citizen, struggling in the recession to care for his or her family, as they read that the Philadelphia Orchestra will spend over $10 million to go through the bankruptcy process. Imagine how that money could be invested in the community. But in this field, it seems there is always money for lawyers. Further, imagine the damage when that same citizen reads that the CEO of a bankrupt orchestra has received a substantial personal salary settlement, which newspaper reports indicate includes a personal financial planner.

Another manager has challenged the jurisdiction of national media contracts, appealing their lost case numerous times and spending who knows how much in legal fees. That money could have funded multiple projects that would have elevated the organization in the mind of the local and international community. Instead, money raised from donors has gone to lawyers.

It is, in a word, outrageous.

Still, some in this room might be wondering how I can overlook the recent bankruptcies in Syracuse and Louisville. The musicians of Syracuse will accomplish what their former management could not, and I have no doubt an orchestra will re-emerge. Louisville is maybe a little different I suppose, because what has been done to the community and the musicians there is even uglier.

In Louisville, an orchestra that has commissioned 120 original compositions and performed over 400 world premieres which served to spread the music of America across the globe is currently functioning as an organization that employs no musicians. It is an orchestra built by the people, and led at its founding by a mayor who believed in the concept of Confucianism that said that a city of high culture with happy citizens will attract wealth, business and power to the city. But now, this historic orchestra looks for musicians on Craigslist and through Facebook ads.

There is not merely one reason for these bankruptcies that can be applied to the entire field. The circumstances are quite different, and in the case of Philadelphia, if you follow a bad real estate deal with an extended period of time without a music director, a CEO, or a board chair, well, can there be any surprise that your organization might get into trouble?

But the negative rhetoric leads to stories that depict a mosaic of failure straight across the heart of America, a tornado traveling I-40 or I-70.

It just isn't true.

What are the solutions? How do we change to preserve the legacy of great music? How do we continue to help educate the next generation of Americans while enhancing the business environment of our cities and elevating the spirits of audiences everywhere.

Well, first we must articulate that we do, in fact, do all of those things!

As ICSOM led at its founding, we intend to lead again into a new era of positive advocacy. To musicians everywhere, I call on you to join us in our positive message of advocacy. It is not enough to simply play your instrument. You must be among your audience, out in the lobby of your concert hall. Shake the hands of your audiences, thank your donors, and welcome them into an environment of community that surrounds every orchestra.

It surely must be clear to musicians by now that no one is going to do this for us. It has been the dedication of the musicians in Honolulu that has led to new orchestral performances in Hawaii. It is the musicians of the former Syracuse Symphony that are keeping the music and the hope alive in Central New York. This is our mission, and we must join together as never before, because something precious is at stake.

To the students of the music school who are here today, I especially ask you to join us. You are the future, and you are not going into a dying field. As you study to be accomplished instrumentalists, you must learn the message of advocacy as well. You must answer the negative messages in our newspapers about the future of orchestras with the truth of what you see. You must tell the story of how music changed your life, of how you have seen it touch other lives, and how communities are forever changed for the better by the presence of a great orchestra.

Should we fail to engage in this effort to tell the real truth, then we are allowing others to define us. It is now officially the job of musicians to introduce themselves to their communities, or they soon might find themselves demonized as the musicians in Louisville have.

I want to emphasize, though, that not everything I am saying applies to "managers" in the abstract. In a speech such as this, one that attempts to focus so diligently on a problem in a way that it has perhaps not been articulated before, it is easy to say "managers" and "musicians". I want to again say clearly that there are many excellent managers, and many of them reach out to their musicians. I am honored when they consult with me on issues that affect their orchestras, eager to share my views on how problems can be avoided, and impressed when they call to ask how to avoid something that could be perceived as negative to the public.

As ICSOM Chair, I have had a unique opportunity to visit with the orchestras of North America, from San Juan to Honolulu. In my visits I meet with the musicians, and visit them in their homes. I am backstage in the lounges, and I hear their rehearsals. I meet with board chairs, staff, and CEOs. I meet the writers who cover the orchestra in the local press. Sometimes I meet the mayors and other political leaders, and I deliver the positive message that our organizations should join together to articulate. It is a rare inside view of our orchestras, and I can see what works and what doesn't.

Places that are working, and are led by great managers, achieve visionary things. They are able to achieve those things because bridges are built between all areas of the organization. The musicians should have access to the board, and everyone should know each other. I am always dismayed when musicians tell me they don't know the staff of their own orchestra. But sometimes, this is due to walls built within the organization. A good manager will foster an environment of collaboration and friendship, and a different kind of manager will inhibit the relationship between musicians and the board.

I hear some board members tell me that they are over-extended as donors, that they cannot give more, and I don't doubt that. I also think that sometimes donors feel under-appreciated by the musicians, which is why the musicians of every orchestra need to establish a way of communicating with their boards and donors, to thank them for their support, and to build friendships.

But while donors may feel pressured in the current economy, too many of our organizations do not create an environment that would expand the donor base by presenting an inviting image to those who might want to become a part of the community that surrounds every symphony orchestra.

There is plenty of money. Despite the economic downturn, the number of millionaires in Metro Detroit, for example, actually increased last year by 4%. In the late 1970s, the wealthiest one per cent of Americans controlled about 9% of the income. Today, that same 1% controls 24% of the nation's income. While a conversation about the sustainability of such a disparity of wealth is of merit, for our field it means that as wealth is more centralized, we must have a message that inspires people to donate and participate. Sadly, we simply lack that message. We cannot expand the donor base with "red alerts" and charts based on faulty data that propose to show a lack of sustainability, as opposed to a vision that demonstrates the possibilities for our orchestras, and the possibilities for their service to reach even more lives. That is the message that will expand the donor base.

But the money is there. When musicians hear their managers tell them that there is no more money in their major metropolitan American communities, they know that their management is really saying that they just can't inspire new donors.

There was a study recently conducted in the Chicago public schools, where three pilot schools of very different socio-economic populations were immersed in an intense arts program. The standardized testing for the schools improved by 12%. No one would protest that music is good for education. Why is that message lost in negativity?

To the students here today, and to musicians everywhere, I urge you to join Americans for the Arts, and you can join their Arts Action Fund free of charge. Americans for the Arts is an advocacy group in

Washington, DC that helps promote positive advocacy on Capitol Hill. When I testified before Congress in 2009 I was joined by their president, Robert Lynch. It is a great organization, and you can help simply by visiting their website.

Musicians have never made greater sacrifices in recognition of economic conditions than they have in the past few years. But too often their sacrifices have been rewarded with scorn. The negative rhetoric must end. We owe better to Beethoven and Bernstein…we owe better to everyone.

We must harvest the frustration that we all are feeling and use it as inspiration. Our spirit will not be defeated, and as artists we will not allow ourselves to fall into the general malaise that seems to be depressing the nation, replacing inspirational words with messages that project only what cannot be achieved instead of what is possible. We must be inspired by the challenge. And we must not hesitate to dream great dreams simply because they are hard to achieve.

When the United States ended the Space Shuttle program recently, I couldn't help but think back fifty years to one of the greatest American speeches ever delivered. On May 25, 1961, John F. Kennedy challenged America to land a man on the moon and return him safely to earth by the end of the decade. On that day he said "While we cannot guarantee that we shall one day be first, we can guarantee that any failure on our part to make these efforts shall make us last." In that speech he said that Americans strive to achieve great things not because they are easy, but because they are hard. He told an Irish folk tale where two young boys on a journey confront a stone wall, too high to mount but too long to circumvent. Facing the prospect of a retreat that would end their adventure, one boy threw the hat of the other over the wall, leaving them no choice to but find some way to overcome this obstacle.

Kennedy spoke in a time when America dreamt of what could be achieved, what could be built, and what could be created. He spoke without any assumption that there was anything that we could not achieve for our children.

America is slowly emerging from the worst of the downturn, and our field is recovering as well. But we cannot withstand another barrage of flawed reports, or another onslaught of negative pronouncements. I ask everyone here to join with ICSOM in celebration of our 50th anniversary as we launch a new era of positive activism and dedication to changing the image of orchestras in America.

To accomplish this we must engage in positive advocacy and education of the public. A recent poll indicated that 40% of Americans believe that as much as 5% of the federal budget goes to support the arts. A shocking 7% of respondents said they thought the government spent half of its budget on arts programs. This is the misconception we deal with in a world of spin where the truth is often a victim of sound bites.

But still, despite this optimism, there are many problems facing us. We must reach out to our communities and inspire them, and no one is ever inspired by ugly language. Should the field fail to hear this call, then we will be left clutching nothing but a fistful of rain. Our colleagues look to those of us in this room for leadership...and to lead, we must offer a message of hope.

The message of hope that we can promote is that orchestras are relevant to the community. Orchestras are an investment, with both financial and educational results for the community. Every orchestra is a family, and every manager has been granted a sacred trust with the community to preserve that family.

The future of this field and the future for live performance of this incredible music is in the hands of everyone here, and in the hands of every musician everywhere. We all can make a difference, and we must know no fear.

At a time when there are many who doubt America's orchestras, we will no longer doubt ourselves. Let us leave here with a renewed spirit of activism, and let us take this message to our colleagues everywhere. This judgment we make affirmatively: if we can change the tone, then we can change the future.

Address to the 2013 Convention of the American Federation of Musicians

LAS VEGAS
JULY 24, 2013

Last week, while visiting with the Boston Symphony at Tanglewood, I made a pilgrimage to the Aaron Copland memorial in the Tanglewood garden where the great composer's ashes are scattered. I was reminded that Copland once said that "To stop the flow of music would be like the stopping of time itself, incredible and inconceivable."

But this season, the flow of music did stop as ICSOM orchestras in Atlanta, Indianapolis, and the Twin Cities were locked out by their boards and managements in an unprecedented and egregious insult to the communities of which these boards claim to be stewards. For the Minnesota Orchestra, the music has yet to return.

Fifty years ago, ICSOM was founded to create a more rewarding livelihood for orchestral performers, and the success of the effort is apparent in concert halls across North America. Our orchestras are now among the very best in the world, and our musicians have earned protections that allow them to care for their families and build upon their artistry as they serve the greater community that surrounds all of our cities. But in a climate of negativity, it could appear that the progress of the past five decades is now at risk.

If one was to believe the negative messages found in the media about orchestras, or the unsupportable claims of imminent disaster that are spewed by some managements and managerial organizations, you might feel a soul-crushing darkness that could lead you to question the validity of hope.

But the good news I bring you today is that the bad news that permeates so many discussions of the future is largely false. Unfortunately though, those false messages can be self-fulfilling, and we must not allow our resolve to be repelled by an assault of damaging words.

The *truth* is that the non-profit arts and culture industry in the United States results in over $135 billion in economic activity every year, and provides over 4 million jobs. The *truth* is that philanthropic giving to the arts reached an all-time high last year of over $14 billion. The *truth* is that the number of businesses contributing to the arts has risen 18% in the past three years.

But these facts are too often dismissed and unheard; and instead they say that orchestras are dying, attendance is declining, and audiences are aging.

Yes, they say that orchestras are dying, but the Houston Symphony approaches its centennial with the momentum of record breaking fundraising, and the San Diego Symphony has seen a decade of balanced finances even as it more than doubled its budget.

Yes, they say that attendance is declining, but the Buffalo Philharmonic sold more subscriptions this year than at any point in its 75-year history, and the Chicago Lyric Opera increased its attendance by 15%.

Yes, they say that audiences are aging, but the Cleveland Orchestra doubled the number of students attending its concerts this year, and is on track to set records for Severance Hall. To even claim that aging audiences are a problem, one must ignore the indisputable fact that life expectancy has increased in this past century at a rate previously unseen in the history of mankind.

At a time of uncertainty in the world, where discord seems more valued than debate, where doctrines of fear and rhetoric of violence replace the inspirational words of hope that have, at moments of past crisis, led the citizens of the world to aspire to something greater than themselves, music has never been more relevant in the lives of people living at a fragile time in a fragile world.

The musicians of ICSOM have never been more united than at this time of difficulty, as challenges always bring a constituency of shared idealism closer when confronted with an assault on what we hold true. We realize that none of the success musicians have cultivated over the past fifty years would have been possible without our united network of friends, and without this union. We also realize that to achieve the greater successes we know are possible, we must be even more united.

We have no claim to condemn the negative messages about our orchestras if we are not doing everything we can to disclaim them. We have no right to refute these messages if we are not doing everything we can to articulate the message of hope that our orchestras provide in the cities where our children learn, our companies do business, and our citizens seek the dignity of building a society based on the principles of humanity.

There is no doubt that times are changing, and we all must be ready to change as well. After all, when I look at my iPhone I know I am holding more technology in my hand than was on the Apollo space crafts that sailed to the moon. Such an astonishing realization creates both opportunities and challenges.

The artist Ai Wei Wei said "The world is changing. This is a fact. Artists work hard hoping to change it according to their own aspirations." He also said "For artists today, what's most needed is to be clear about social responsibility."

The next generation of musicians will build careers that are different from the careers of their teachers. This next generation must be the most ardent advocates that music has ever known, and we must provide the example for them to build upon just as those who went before built the foundation of unionism for us.

Every means available should be utilized; every opportunity of technology should be explored. The delegates in this convention hall should become a sodality of Tweeters, of Facebookers; skilled in any area of social media that can relay the positive and truthful messages that will enhance our chance of success while negating the messages of those who seek to approach the future by turning back the clock.

ICSOM comprises 4000 musicians. In the context of the total membership of the AFM, that may seem a relatively small number. But for the impact that our orchestras have on our communities and within our Locals, our presence is unmistakable. Our dedication to this union is demonstrated by the financial support we provide to our Locals. Indeed, in many cases, our orchestras sustain our Locals. We have always been there for this union, and now in this time of economic difficulty, we know the union will be there for us as well.

If it is true that what is most needed is to be clear about social responsibility, then we must lead by example in a tireless way that will inspire our colleagues and our communities. The musicians of the world look to those of us in this room for leadership, and we will answer that call. Boards that would seek to silence music through lockouts are displaying a shocking lack of social responsibility, but we will answer any such negative and false message with a positive and true message of hope. Virtue and vice must not receive the same reward, and our true opponent is frustration, and our true enemy is apathy.

The musicians of ICSOM and the musicians of this union will not allow a destructive message to undermine our idealism and hope, and we will not validate the words of those we do not respect. Those who question the value of our music cannot make us question our heart, and at a time when there are some who doubt our orchestras, we will not doubt ourselves. The comfort we can take in a time of difficulty comes from the indisputable truth that the positive message offered by musicians will far outlast the negativity of those that seek to silence us.

Music *cannot* be silenced, and music *will not* be silenced. As Aaron Copland said, to do so would be inconceivable. We will stand together, as always, in solidarity. And if we do, there can be no doubt that we will all gather together again in unity to celebrate many future successes.

Address to the 3ʳᵈ International Orchestra Conference of the Federation International des Musiciens

FEBRUARY 22, 2014
OSLO, NORWAY

Fourteen days ago, President Obama nominated a new chairperson for the National Endowment for the Arts. The musicians of the International Conference of Symphony and Opera Musicians (ICSOM), welcome the nomination of Jane Chu, as we lobbied vigorously for the President to take this action. The President waited 13 regrettable months though before he even made a nomination. The position stood vacant for all of that time, even as some members of Congress called for massive cuts in the National Endowment for the Arts (NEA) in an attempt to weaken the agency.

The NEA was established in 1965 and is dedicated to bringing the arts to all Americans. But since its founding, the NEA has been a constant target for political attacks.

There is a misperception that the U.S. Government spends a great deal on arts funding, but the reality is that only 0.066% of the federal budget is invested in the arts. And for that feeble investment, there is a considerable return. Each dollar the government invests in the arts returns over $7 dollars to the community.

American orchestras are non-profit, tax exempt organizations. In 1966, just a year after the creation of the NEA, another organization, the National Football League (NFL), was also granted non-profit status by the U.S. Government. American Football is very popular, and the NFL generates almost $10 billion in annual revenue and pays its commissioner a yearly salary over $44 million. A 30-second advertisement during this year's Super Bowl cost $4 million. But as a non-profit organization, the NFL pays no taxes.

This is not meant as an attack on the NFL. Like many Americans, I was raised in an environment where football was part of every Sunday afternoon, but the incongruity between a non-profit that earns almost $10 billion a year and an arts organization that struggles to survive must be noted as simply absurd and indicative of how government undervalues the arts.

Politicians in our country bemoan the descending ranking of our education system, yet multiple studies reveal the value of the arts in enhancing our children's future. Despite evidence indicating the need to invest in the arts, our federal and local governments continue to cut the arts in schools.

But let's continue the comparison of non-profits by looking at the budgets for our ICSOM orchestras. The $44 million annual salary of the football commissioner alone surpasses the annual individual budgets of 40 ICSOM member orchestras. In fact, just two minutes of commercial airtime during the Super Bowl broadcast surpasses the budgets of 12 of our ICSOM orchestras.

In America, orchestras have faced a time of difficulty as we emerge from the recession. The troubles have been widely reported, and even more widely misreported. There have been some terrible situations, with an unprecedented lockout in Minnesota, and the bankruptcy of the New York City Opera among others. But the true story to be told is how resilient our orchestras have been, with many orchestras achieving record fundraising and increased attendance. This is true in Cleveland, Houston, Los Angeles, St. Louis, Chicago, Buffalo and many other cities.

Unfortunately, the media loves a negative story and the many successes have been drowned out by the relatively few failures. This false negativity hurts us all, and damages our ability to change the minds of politicians who are too eager to accept stereotypical statements such as "classical music is dead." Some journalists have been writing that same story for over 60 years.

The good news I bring you today is that the bad news that permeates so many discussions of the future is largely false. Unfortunately, though, those false messages can be self-fulfilling and too easily believed by political leaders.

We must not be dissuaded by these negative self-promoting voices. We have a message of hope for the world and we must find ways to be heard. This will require political astuteness and unity among all musicians. We must harvest the power of social networking to advocate any cause that musicians in any country might face. We must recognize that our true opponent is frustration, and our true enemy is apathy.

Those who spread negative messages claim that our audiences are aging beyond retrieval, but The Cleveland Orchestra has doubled the number of students attending its concerts, and I continue to see an infusion of youth in concert halls all over the world. To claim that aging audiences create an insurmountable problem, one must ignore that, in 1940, life expectancy was 62 years. Today it is 79 years. If we accept that people generally tend to turn towards attending symphonic concerts after they have reached a point of greater leisure in their lives, then the fact that we have our target audience for an additional 17 years of life is not a problem, it is an opportunity.

A positive note from the recent NFL Super Bowl was the pre-game performance of Renee Fleming. Ms. Fleming was the first opera singer to be selected for this event, and millions of people were exposed to her luminous voice, many for the first time. Musicians should launch a campaign to encourage major sporting events in all countries to feature more opera singers, and more classical instrumentalists. We might not succeed everywhere, but the campaign would garner much needed positive attention.

Governments will be influenced only by the activism of the people they govern, so we must together raise our voices in a media-savvy manner, and advocate as aggressively for our orchestras, our music schools, and our art form as those with billions of dollars at their disposal will advocate maintaining the non-profit status of the NFL.

In a world that occasionally slumps with the weight of its burdens, we have a universally inspiring message. Wherever a negative image of the arts is produced, by politicians, journalists, or anyone, musicians across the world must be prepared to respond with our positive message of hope.

In times of negativity, we will not be dissuaded from what we hold true. We must rage against the dying of the light. We must be our own advocates, strengthened with the knowledge that the best of humanity is on our side.

Opening Address to the 2014 ICSOM Conference

We have often marveled (and occasionally despaired) at the fact that we work in a field where all too often organizational failure is accepted, and all too often such failure is even expected. For me, this has never been more strikingly illustrated than in the recent announcement from the management of the Green Bay Symphony, a member of ROPA, that it would close following this next season despite several recent profitable years.

The executive director publicly labeled the profitable years "a fluke." What other business would do that? Well...no other business. Successful businesses would highlight the profits, knowing that success breeds success. No business would dismiss profits as "a fluke" thereby suggesting that their successes had nothing to do with the quality of the product, the excellence of the employees, or the importance of the service to the community.

Too often our field continues to attribute organizational failure to the ever-impending "death of classical music." But other businesses face difficulties too. After all, it is said that 90% of restaurants in America fail in their first year of business, yet no one would claim that Americans no longer like to eat.

But in a field where organizational failure is too often accepted, even expected, it seems amazing that so many orchestras can be overcoming such suppositions to be performing so well, especially in these economic times. Such successes are being experienced in places with positive expectations, and in life what you expect is often what you will get. If you find failure to be a reasonable result, and you spread such a message, then negative results are often what your vision will deliver. If you sow the wind, then you are certain to reap the whirlwind.

As we review the orchestral season, it is clear that difficulties remain, and it is clearer still that there will be a few storms ahead. But what is even more apparent is that, if success is a fluke, there certainly have been a lot of "fluky" things going on for orchestras and the arts.

- The Chicago Symphony received the two largest gifts in its history, totaling $32 million
- The Indianapolis Symphony saw a 19% surge in ticket sales with an increase of 30% in subscription sales.
- The Cleveland Orchestra announced a balanced budget, growing audiences, increased endowment, and a record number of student attendees
- The Lyric Opera of Chicago, which has operated in the black for 26 of the past 27 seasons, saw significant increases in revenue and fundraising, and an increase of 8% in ticket sales
- The city of New York City increased funding for arts in the public schools by $23 million, and is expected to hire 120 additional arts teachers
- As Symphoria works heroically to establish a great and permanent orchestral presence in Syracuse in the wake of the unnecessary Syracuse Symphony bankruptcy, the new orchestra is now receiving grants, including funding for its educational mission
- The San Antonio Symphony celebrated its 75th anniversary as it prepares to move into its new home, the Tobin Center
- The Florida Orchestra saw an increase in attendance of 30%
- The Houston Symphony's gala raised over $2.5 million in one evening for education programs on the heels of consecutive tears of record breaking fundraising
- The New York City Ballet's Spring Gala Celebrated Fifty Years at Lincoln Center and raised $3.15 Million
- The Milwaukee Symphony reached a goal of $5 million dollars from new donors

- The Cincinnati Symphony's endowment has grown by 43% and the number of gifts has increased by 94%, leading to a double-digit increase in attendance
- The Grand Rapids Symphony launched a $40 million endowment drive with a $20 million gift
- The Detroit Symphony's holiday concerts set a new box office record just one year after seeing a 43% increase in donations
- The Buffalo Philharmonic saw an 11.9% surge in contributions, endowment growth of 7.7%, and an increase in ticket sales with records set for subscriptions

In previous conferences we have come together to rally support for the musicians of Hawaii, and this month the Hawaii Symphony has ratified a new two-year union agreement and has just announced programming for its third season.

And in Louisville, where in 2011 the board sought to replace their great musicians through ads on Craigslist, that legendary orchestra now approaches a new season with a new manager, a new music director, a new Local union president, a budget surplus, and new donors who have given over $5 million.

I have been traveling the world over the past decade spreading the message that for every story of failure there are ten stories of success for the arts, all the while hoping that we could sow the seeds of positive advocacy that could lead to a new era of artistic relevance for the modern world. I was recently inspired by a quote from Gustav Mahler, who said:

"I am hitting my head against the walls, but the walls are giving way."

Many of these successes might not have been possible if not for the friendship that exists among musicians throughout the world. I have often referred to ICSOM as a "United Network of Friends" and that is indeed what we are. The response to ICSOM's numerous Calls to Action, to raise funds to support our musicians in need, has been remarkable. More than that, it has been reassuring and inspiring. The response to our Call to Action to support the Locked Out Musicians of the Minnesota Orchestra gave tremendous and tangible support to their effort, and their efforts were indeed made on behalf of all us. With the recent attention to the negotiations at the Metropolitan Opera, I was already being asked by our members how they could donate to support the musicians. When we support our friends we are truly investing in our own orchestras and our own families as well.

One of my most moving moments of this past season came on January 14, while in Tampa. I walked into a meeting of the committees of the Florida Orchestra, and they handed me a check for $800 to send to the Minnesota Orchestra musicians. What I knew at that time, but couldn't quite reveal for another hour or so, was on that day the most egregious lockout in the history of orchestras had finally ended.

As uplifting as the response to these Calls to Action has been, we nonetheless hope we never have to issue another. But we know we will, and we know we must remain prepared to support any musician in need. We must remain vigilant because we don't know what might occur even in these next few weeks. But, as we gather here today in Los Angeles, we commence our discussions on a day on which no orchestra is locked out.

Numerous issues still await our collective action. Problems large and small face musicians and arise on a weekly basis. We must respond always, unified, and without apathy or any sense of futility.

Musicians who travel abroad are now faced with a difficult decision regarding their instruments which, through no fault of their own, may contain minuscule amounts of ivory. I want to speak very clearly about this issue: we deplore the despicable poaching of elephants which, in this day, is done almost entirely by a criminal element; a criminal element that funds terrorism. Recent reports show that the elephant population has reached a terrible tipping point, where more elephants are being slaughtered for their tusks then are being born. This must stop. While practically no instrument maker today still uses ivory in the manufacture of instruments, we nonetheless call for an end to the use of ivory in the crafting of any new instrument.

However, it is simply a fact that many of our antique instruments were made with small amounts of ivory at a time when it was completely legal. As we call on the citizens of the world to work to stop this poaching, we also ask our government to recognize that this slaughter perpetrated by terrorists cannot be stopped by launching initiatives that serve to punish musicians by putting their instruments, and therefore their livelihoods, at risk.

We ask every member of ICSOM to write to their congressional delegations, expressing support for initiatives that serve to protect all endangered species, but also asking that reasonableness be applied in the evaluation of our cherished and irreplaceable instruments.

When we act together our voices will be heard as clearly as our music.

I have been reading a book this summer on how the internet and tools such as Twitter have changed how we all communicate and organize. The impact on world events has been immeasurable. In the revolution that overthrew Hosni Mubarak, Egyptians armed with little more than smartphones in their pocket rose up together through communications on Twitter, and they accomplished a revolution in a country where you needed a permit from the government to gather in groups larger than five.

When Nigerian schoolchildren were kidnapped by the despicable terrorists of Boko Haram, the world became aware through a Twitter hashtag campaign, and in a matter of hours a group that was previously unknown to most of the world was exposed, and now the world must be charged to act.

Authoritarian governments use three techniques to suppress the spirits of the people they attempt to control. They use isolation, fear, and apathy.

Through isolation they intend to keep the like-minded citizens of the world from organizing.

Through fear they intend to suppress the actions of the people through the knowledge of what might happen to them should they dare to rise.

And apathy is really futility. They create a sense of "what can I do? I am just one person."

By no means do I intend to compare these horrific world events with the plight of the artist in North America, but it occurs to me that these same techniques are used by less nefarious factions to control the thinking of a people. In the battle for advocacy of our place as artists and musicians in society, there is an attempt to keep us isolated, to keep us fearful, and to keep us apathetic.

At this time of darkness for the world, music remains an inextinguishable light. Where others respond with vitriol we respond with music, and where others respond with violence, again we respond with music.

As the current border crisis expands, there are many who have responded by carrying accusatory signs and shouting epithets of hatred and division. But the musicians of the San Diego Symphony responded by joining with the musicians of the Orquesta Baja California to play Bach on opposite sides of a border fence in a profound demonstration of peace in a very noisy world.

We will not be isolated. We will not be fearful. We will not be apathetic.

We must not listen to the negative voices, and we must never doubt ourselves or the role we play in a society that yearns for relief from the destructive rhetoric that bombards us all from the ideologues that dominate the media. They are profiting from the division they sow.

I was recently amazed when I saw an audacious commercial promoting Koch Industries that claimed that they employ 60,000 Americans. Well, the arts employ over 4 million Americans, yet the role of the artist is seemingly forever diminished.

Currently ICSOM is building what we believe is the most important Twitter feed in classical music. We have over 6000 followers, and that allows us to spread our message instantly around the world, but we need 10,000 followers, we need 15,000. We must use this tool to spread the importance of the arts in education, in health, in financial impact, and in the elevation of the human spirit at a time when inspiration is harder and harder to find. Musicians must deliver that inspiration to a slumping world, and we will.

The work for ICSOM and on behalf of musicians across the world can be exhausting, and on many nights I find my writing interrupted by the sunrise. The light of the day often greets me while I am still absorbed with the darkness of the night.

On August 11, I was returning to North Carolina from Dallas following multiple trips on behalf of ICSOM, and, having arrived at the airport early, I fell asleep at the gate, not more than ten feet from the door to the jetway. Apparently I slept more deeply and for much longer than I intended. Eventually I awoke to music in my head, which almost inexplicably it seemed to me, was *Old Man River*. I lingered for a moment in that place between sleep and wake, not really knowing where I was, until I saw that the shoeshine guy across the hallway was indeed singing, *Old Man River*. But that reverie was then interrupted with the announcement

"Passenger Ridge, door closing in 15 seconds." I jumped right away, saying "I'm right here. Weren't you even going to hold a mirror under my nose or anything?"

But I as ran to the jetway, I turned back to hear a bit more of *Old Man River*, but instead saw a CNN TV monitor with the words "Robin Williams dead; apparent suicide."

I boarded the plane, barely awake and confused. It was a dark flight. On that day in the world, there were people trapped on a mountainside in Iraq, facing a terrorist onslaught. War had escalated again in the Middle East. Protests of racial injustice had begun in Ferguson, Missouri, which I knew would inevitably lead to more violence. And now, Robin Williams was dead.

That day reminded me of a song on Simon and Garfunkel's third album. The song has the two voices singing *Silent Night* as a news program softly plays in the background. The words of the reporter slowly rise in the mix as the music grows softer. The news that is reported is the actual news of another day in August, some 48 years earlier. The stories that are read (in contrast to the strains of "sleep in peace") include:

- Opposition to the Civil Rights Bill
- A report that the National Guard would be called should Martin Luther King hold a rally just outside of Chicago
- Escalation of the war in Vietnam
- Investigation of protestors of the war by the House Un-American Activities Committee
- And, the death of comedian Lenny Bruce

There has always been darkness in the world, and there always will be; but there has also always been music. Many in our network of friends are still reeling from the terrible event that occurred in Chautauqua last week where a musician lost her life to an act of senseless violence, and while there can be no logical explanation for this or these other events, we will still respond with music.

As Leonard Bernstein famously said just after the assassination of President Kennedy:

"This sorrow and rage will not inflame us to seek retribution; rather they will inflame our art. Our music will never again be quite the same. This will be our reply to violence: to make music more intensely, more beautifully, more devotedly than ever before"

Our music has never been more relevant to a world that slumps with the weight of its burdens. Our friendships with each other have never been closer or more needed. Those of us in this network of friends have a shared legacy, a shared childhood, a shared present, and a shared future. Whether we realize it or not we have never been more powerful than we are right now. And while it is a dark world, it is also a beautiful world. And we add beauty to this world every time we walk on stage with our colleagues, knowing that our friends across North America are walking on to their stage as well at the very same time to spread the very same message of hope.

Our conference theme is *The Art of Advocacy*, and this coming year we will pursue that art as vigorously as we pursue the art of music. It will only be through the art of advocacy that we will achieve our expectation of a thriving musical and cultural society across North America and throughout the world. When others merely talk about what is *sustainable*, we will talk about what is *achievable*. When others say what can't be done, musicians will demonstrate what *is* possible by joining together through our united network of friends to spread our message of hope.

Those of you who know me best must realize that there is a certain irony in my standing before you to dispute that it is a dark and tragic world, and yet that is exactly my purpose here today and it is also the reason that I have decided to stand for re-election to an unprecedented fifth term as chair of this historic organization. Should the delegates see fit to re-elect me, I promise to take this message across the world as eagerly I have over these past eight years. For every time a TV monitor in an airport lounge tells me some bad news, I think of my thousands of friends who on a daily basis achieve astonishing things that represent the very best of humanity.

I think of the Musicians of the Minnesota Orchestra, who stood together against powerful people who sought to break their spirit and in doing so emerged closer and stronger.

I think of the negotiating committee of the Metropolitan Opera Orchestra, who orchestrated a magnificent public relations campaign and stood together in the face of overwhelming worldwide news coverage as their management sought to break their will.

I think of the musicians of the Louisville Orchestra that worked against great odds, standing together to literally save their orchestra.

I think of the musicians of Syracuse, who in creating Symphoria are seeking to achieve something their previous board leaders refused to even attempt.

As I have served in this role, I have been moved and inspired by every musician I have met. On overnight flights back to North Carolina I never travel alone. I am always accompanied by the music from every concert I have heard and every rehearsal I have attended.

We will not be isolated. We will not be fearful. We will not be apathetic.

This is not a time to feel darkness for the world. This is a time for all of us to bring light to the souls that we know are burdened. It is not too trite to say "We *are* the music makers and we *are* the dreamers of dreams." We must not doubt ourselves, or allow negative voices to influence us. We must never validate the words of those we do not respect. It is crucial that we all allow ourselves to recall the amazement we felt when we were learning music for the first time, and when we knew nothing of the negativity that sometime surrounds our field.

We will greet any doubts with a unified message of hope. We will stand in favor of any positive message, and we will continue to care for each other as the united network of friends that we are. It is fatiguing to always feel that we are working against something, or trying to prevent something. In this week together, we will talk about things to work <u>for</u> and positive visions that we can imagine and achieve.

In this week, and in this coming year, as always, I will again be counting on you for inspiration.

We will not be isolated. We will not be fearful. We will not be apathetic. The world will hear our voices just as they have always heard our music. I look forward to continuing our work together in this cause.

Address to the 2016
Convention of the American
Federation of Musicians

JUNE 20, 2016
LAS VEGAS

In October of 1963, President Kennedy set forth his vision for the future of the arts when he spoke at Amherst College, saying:

> *"I see little of more importance to the future of our country and our civilization than full recognition of the place of the artist. I look forward to an America which will reward achievement in the arts as we reward achievement in business or statecraft. I look forward to an America which will steadily raise the standards of artistic accomplishment and which will steadily enlarge cultural opportunities for all of our citizens."*

Kennedy's inspiring message, delivered less than a month before his tragic assassination, recognized the value of the artist in society, and yet more than fifty years later we have to ask ourselves if his vision has been realized. In so many ways it appears his words have been neglected, and the greatest threat to a growing future for the arts in America is the persistent and often unchallenged negative rhetoric *about* the future of the arts in America.

This negative view has been around a very long time. We have articles with headlines that proclaim "25 Symphonies Doomed to Die" which would be of more concern if the articles were not published in 1970 and if not for the fact that all the orchestras destined for doom remain vital today.

We have a document written by the president of the board of the Chicago Symphony, who said:

> "The (Chicago Symphony) now must solve a problem which has arisen from economic conditions beyond its control. A deficit has been incurred, and undoubtedly there will be annual deficits for some years to come. This affects the future of the orchestra...(and) our problem does not differ in kind from the financial problem that faces each of the major orchestras in the United States."

This is especially troubling isn't it? ...that an orchestra as great as the Chicago Symphony could face this predicament. I would be more alarmed had this not been written in April, 1940.

Despite this, our orchestras continue to thrive in a difficult economic environment. This season alone, the musicians of the Baltimore Symphony earned a 6.4% raise, and the musicians of the Kansas City Symphony earned raises that amount to nearly 20% over the term of their new contract. The Indianapolis Symphony received a $10 million gift and the New York Philharmonic received a $25 million dollar gift. The Omaha Symphony saw record breaking attendance, and the Chicago Symphony saw record breaking ticket sales.

The latest studies show that charitable giving to the arts rose 6.8% in 2015. Music is now a part of federal education policy, the economic impact of the arts for our cities is widely recognized, music therapy is increasingly being accepted as treatment for numerous medical conditions, and soon an opera singer, Marian Anderson, will be honored on United States currency.

And yet, seemingly inexplicably, the negative perception remains.

The musicians of ICSOM's newest member, the Grand Rapids Symphony, recently completed a year-long negotiation, one where they fought off potentially devastating cuts by utilizing new techniques and mastering public relations messages that served to win the support of the entire community and change the negative viewpoints of their board.

The musicians accomplished this all while building positive relationships that will serve them well into the future, and which led to the successful completion of a $40 million endowment campaign. But when this news was reported in the press, the articles began by declaring that other orchestras across the country are in decline, while offering no evidence of the veracity of such a misleading statement. Even articles that report on the incredible growth of the Los Angeles Philharmonic have begun with the same statement, as if somehow false negativity is a mandated doctrine of the press that covers our orchestras.

In this decade the musicians of ICSOM have endured numerous labor disputes, and outlasted a terrible recession. But they have not just endured, they have grown. They have stood against negativity, cultivated new techniques for negotiation and advocacy, and led the way in demonstrating how music is an inherent call for peace and inclusiveness. Increasingly our musicians are producing their own concerts that raise money for the hungry, provide inspiration for the homeless, and advance healing for the sick.

In an all-too-often violent world, the musicians of ICSOM stand united in proclaiming that every note we play, every lesson we teach, every concert we perform is a statement against violence and a statement for unity and peace in the world.

We believe we have brought this unity to ICSOM by articulating ideals to work *for* instead of only offering problems to work *against*, and we have sought to share this unity with the entire AFM. The musicians of ICSOM are nearly 99% organized, a claim that we doubt any other segment of this union could make. All the more remarkable is that this has been achieved even though 36% of our orchestras are in so-called "Right to Work" states. One must wonder if such orchestral solidarity with the AFM would be possible were it not for ICSOM.

When ICSOM tries to alert the leadership of the AFM to issues and problems that could prove divisive if not addressed, it is the most *pro-union* endeavor a member could undertake. But too often in recent years, our messages to the leadership of the union have occasionally been met with resistance. When we are visiting with the orchestral members of the AFM from San Juan to Honolulu, from Halifax to Victoria, we are learning the concerns and issues that affect the health of our orchestras, and the health of the families of our members.

To our members, it seems inconceivable that anyone could doubt that ICSOM is the best friend the AFM could ever have.

We must embrace our future as eagerly as we celebrate our past. To achieve anything in life you must first imagine it, and we can imagine a union that is stronger.

Imagine a union where our membership is growing and not declining. Imagine a union that inspires its members with a message of hope and inclusiveness that galvanizes musicians to want to join and participate. Imagine a union that stands as a beacon of peace and beauty in a time of universal unrest.

We must embrace new media, we must embrace new ideals, we must embrace new technologies, and we must be on the forefront of the astute and thoughtful use of the tools that the modern world has provided us.

We live in a media-driven world, where community relations campaigns are an essential part of any negotiation. Embracing new tools does not represent a surrender of tradition or solidarity; it represents a crucial step in the preservation of our many institutions. As the great composer Gustav Mahler once wrote, "Tradition is not the worship of ashes, but the preservation of fire." Should we fail to offer this message of hope to our members and to the entire world, we will be left clutching nothing more than a fistful of rain.

In our troubled world, a world that often slumps with the weight of its burdens, humanity will always persevere in the face of violence, and music will forever be a response to hatred. The great violinist Bronislaw Huberman, a man responsible for saving thousands of Jewish musicians from the Holocaust through the creation of the Palestine Symphony, once wrote that "The true artist does not create art as an end in itself. He creates art for human beings. Humanity is the goal."

Imagine a union that spreads this message of hope far beyond its membership. That is the union I imagined in those early days in Norfolk, Virginia, when I was 15 years old and my teachers took me to get my first union card at Local 125. Now, as I prepare to step away from my position as Chair of ICSOM this August, a position I have been honored to hold longer than anyone before me, a union of hope remains the union I imagine is possible to achieve.

I want to thank you all for the friendship and support you have shown me in this decade. After all of this time I still believe even more deeply in the message of hope that ICSOM has articulated for this union. I have no doubt that by effectively articulating a vision of the hope for the world that all music provides, and by standing as a beacon of peace, and by truly inspiring our members as the united network of friends that they are, the AFM can become the union that we all have always imagined.

Final Address to ICSOM

It is a great pleasure to be with you all again. I am very excited about this week. And as the week progresses even more friends will be joining us. But as excited as I am about this week I am even more excited about the future.

It is meaningful that we are gathering here today in our nation's Capital at a time of decision for our country, and a time of unrest for the world. Just two miles from here, the memorial for Martin Luther King stands with his words forever carved in granite to remind us of some of his most powerful aspirations for the world. There we are reminded that Dr. King once said "I have the audacity to believe that people everywhere can have three meals a day for their bodies, education and culture for their minds, and dignity, equality, and freedom for their spirits."

This will be the final time that I speak before you as ICSOM Chair to open our annual conference. It is impossible to avoid feeling sentimental at moments of transition in life, and as I speak here today I am certainly not immune from nostalgia.

It was never my intention to become ICSOM Chair. I have been a professional musician since I was 15, and the timing of my early career was such that I was able to meet many of our greatest leaders of the past, and then work with the great leaders of the present. But time only moves in one direction, and I am now privileged to know the musicians who will become the greatest leaders of our future.

Being here in Washington today makes me reflect back well over thirty-five years, when I would come here to study with the principal bassist of the National Symphony, Steve Brewster. I began before I had a driver's license, so my parents would drive me four hours each way from Virginia Beach for lessons every other week. I think that at the time I didn't fully recognize the sacrifice they were making in surrendering an entire day of their lives so frequently just to assist my studies. It is impossible to state how much I wish they were still here, but if they were I hope that they might feel that I have done something with my life to earn such incredible support.

But a little over ten years ago, I was convinced by members of the Governing Board to become more involved in ICSOM, especially Brian Rood and Richard Levine during a fateful cab ride to the airport in Pittsburgh. They convinced me that there was a need to change, and I had seen it as well. The pervasive outlook for the future of our orchestras was dim, relationships throughout the field were fractured, the members of our orchestras were not caring for each other and standing with each other in an empathetic way, and many within our own organization were questioning the relevance of ICSOM.

When we began this effort over ten years ago, orchestras faced a constant barrage of negativity, and while some of that remains we have found ways to work together to articulate a different message…a message of hope for the future of our orchestras in our communities. That message has been largely successful.

In recent weeks I have been reviewing some of my statements from my earliest speeches as Chair, and it's interesting to compare what we said we were going to do with what we have actually achieved.

In 2006 I said:

> For too long the messages in our orchestras' glossy brochures have conflicted with the messages in our inky newspapers. I would suggest to you that musicians have been losing the public relations war, and we must proclaim now that we will no longer cede that victory…
>
> Where it is asked "how can our community continue to support the arts" the answer must be, resoundingly, "How can we afford not to?"…

This will be the focus of ICSOM over these next few years. We will work to spread the message… that …where the arts are concerned…the greater the investment, the greater the return.

We must work to make this truth more apparent, and for that…the responsibility falls on our shoulders.

The negative rhetoric about our industry must change, and we are the ones to change it and mold it into a positive message that we can spread to our constituencies and communities. Our orchestras can serve as beacons of hope and symbols of excellence in a world that is too often without hope and too often content with mediocrity.

While it is and has always been so in vogue for orchestral musicians to be cynical, it is not beyond us to continue to indulge in our dreams. The greatest musicians among us are those who are still inspired by the opportunity to inspire. Through uniting together and reaching out to our communities, we can and will ensure that the arts continue to thrive, and we will enrich the lives of our audiences while inspiring the next generation of musicians.

So, those words are now a decade old, but I think they reflect much of what we have done together. We started talking about beauty…we started using expressions like "a united network of friends." We swore that we would not be isolated, we would not be fearful, we would not be apathetic. We talked about what was possible more than what was not. And while others spoke of what was sustainable, we spoke of what was achievable.

Perhaps most importantly, we were not too inhibited to talk about our hopes and we were not too shy to talk about our dreams. Indeed the musicians of ICSOM have become so unified that it is almost difficult to remember that there was ever a time when were not.

This friendship and unity has been most visibly on display through the incredible generosity of our members through the multiple Calls to Action that have been issued. Through these Calls we have sustained musicians and their families in times of terrible crisis. Whenever we asked, you all responded. I think Bob Marley might have said that "You never know how strong you are until being strong is your only choice." In this decade the musicians of our orchestras have endured numerous labor disputes, and outlasted a terrible recession. But we have not just endured, we have grown. We have stood against negativity, cultivated new techniques for negotiation and advocacy, and led the way in demonstrating how music is an inherent call for peace and inclusiveness.

Who can forget the negative pronouncements that accompanied the Detroit Symphony strike in 2010? So many in the press claimed that the city of Detroit could no longer support a world class orchestra, and those of us who were more optimistic were accused by pundits across the world of being resistant to change and determined to embrace only the status quo.

Who could have envisioned that just six years later the Detroit Symphony would have a budget surplus, an increase in subscription revenue, and individual donations of millions of dollars? Who could have envisioned that the relationships would become so strong that a donor would leave a $5000 gift for every member of the orchestra in her will?

The musicians of North America could envision it, and we did envision it, and we were right.

Much success has been achieved by our orchestras, and in this season alone:

- The Atlanta Symphony recorded its second budget surplus in a row
- The Baltimore Symphony received a $6 million gift earmarked for education and the musicians received substantial raises
- The Buffalo Philharmonic received a $1 million gift
- The Chicago Symphony saw its fifth consecutive year of record-breaking ticket sales
- The Cleveland Orchestra reported a surplus, endowment growth, and larger audiences
- The Florida Orchestra eliminated its debt, and raised its endowment to $17 million
- The Grand Rapids Symphony reached its $40 million endowment goal

- The Indianapolis Symphony received a $10 million gift and reported its third straight year of balanced budgets, with increased revenue, contributions, and subscriptions
- The Jacksonville Symphony increased ticket sales by 9%
- The Kansas City Symphony set all-time records for attendance and the musicians earned raises that amount to nearly 20% over the term of their contract
- The Nashville Symphony musicians earned a raise of 10.9% over two years
- The New York Philharmonic announced a $25 million gift on opening night
- St. Louis Symphony saw increases in ticket sales, revenue, endowment and contributions

In the United States, the latest studies show that charitable giving to the arts rose 6.8% in 2015. Music is now a part of federal education policy, the economic impact of the arts for our cities is widely recognized, music therapy is increasingly being accepted as treatment for numerous medical conditions, and soon an opera singer, Marian Anderson, will be honored on United States currency.

But it hasn't all been successful, and many issues still weigh heavily on my thoughts. When I assumed this role I believed that we could build bridges across all areas of the field, but the chasms have proven deeper and wider than I imagined. Among our managements, the corporate mind-set of too many of our boards is in conflict with the artistic aspirations of our musicians, and even with the missions of the orchestras they are charged to maintain.

I have always believed, though, that consensus can be reached, and solutions can be found among those who are really seeking them.

In Asheville, North Carolina, there is a rock-climbing wall on one of the downtown streets, but they don't want you climbing it at night, so there is a five-foot fence around it that they lock up. I've looked at that fence many times on many evenings, and thought "if you think you can climb that wall, then that fence isn't going to be much of a problem." I've tried to apply that lesson to our work. Sometimes we never reach the largest obstacles because the initial barriers are too much of a nuisance to surmount.

We must continue to elevate our efforts, and we will face new difficulties. Even now, we must stand ready to assist the Musicians of the Fort Worth Symphony as they work valiantly for a fair contract that reflects the growth of their city and maintains the widely acknowledged excellence of their orchestra. And we can unfortunately be certain that difficulties for other orchestras will emerge as well, some as early as this fall. I have no doubt that the musicians of ICSOM will be as eager to stand with their friends and colleagues in the coming years as they have over this past decade. I am confident that the next generation of ICSOM leadership will take the organization to its greatest heights, and tremendous success awaits the next Chairperson.

"International" has always been part of our organization's name, and when we began in 1962 we did have international members. But in recent years ICSOM has built and renewed friendships with musicians across the world, and I am very excited that at this conference we will welcome friends from Amsterdam, London, Paris, as well as Canada and Australia. This is especially important, as the world stands at a moment of turmoil, and the need for the activism of musicians everywhere is great. From the floods of Louisiana to wars in Aleppo to attacks on the streets of European capitals, the citizens of the world are in need of unity, of comfort, and of generosity.

In recent years my thoughts have turned to the role that music plays for all of humanity, especially as we have seen the world slump in moments of turmoil and violence. I have been constantly reminded of the words of the great violinist Bronislaw Huberman, a man responsible for saving thousands of Jewish musicians from the Holocaust, who said that "The true artist does not create art as an end in itself. He creates art for human beings. Humanity is the goal."

Now in modern times we are bombarded with the negative and so often destructive words of political candidates and the media. I know that there will always be opportunists that place personal ambition over service to others, but the portrait they consistently paint of the world is so drastic and self-serving that they seem to suggest that our only options are a choice between immorality and lunacy.

An article I read earlier this year among the din of political analysis reminded me of the choices the world now faces. At times of crisis, the article said, leaders tend to emerge that "...lead people to feel they have lost control of their country and destiny, people look for scapegoats, a charismatic leader captures the popular mood, and singles out that scapegoat. He talks in rhetoric that has no detail, and drums up anger and hatred."

This plays into what another writer has called "The Persuasive Power of Repeated Falsehoods." Musicians face these "repeated falsehoods" everywhere we look. Our orchestras are not dying, music is not losing its relevance, the world is not beyond hope, and humanity will persevere.

Yesterday, at Central Union Mission, we again stood for humanity as we served and performed for those who were both hungry and in need of solace, too often neglected by our society. This is no small gesture. Musicians must seek ways to serve our communities, and by doing so at our annual meetings we will inspire the colleagues in our orchestras to do so throughout the year, and we will inspire our audiences with our actions just as we have always inspired them with our music.

That is how to respond to terrorism, that is how to respond to violence, that is how to respond to hunger, and discrimination, and injustice.

I, too, see the world in a time of crisis but I see it differently than those candidates or those media pundits, all of whom profit from the division that they sow.

In June in Orlando, a man with an unspeakable weapon, unimaginable to America's founding fathers, killed 49 people and wounded many others in a vicious attack on the LGBT community and an attack on all the values we aspire to uphold. The actions of one destroyed the lives of many, but in contrast to that one, many thousands lined up to donate blood, and no doubt saved additional lives. There are always more people that want to help than want to hurt.

It is easy to see only the destructive people, but even while under assault there remains more kindness in this world than misanthropy.

Perhaps I can be somewhat more optimistic because of who I have spent my time with in the past ten years. I have spent ten years surrounding myself with the musicians of our orchestras, musicians who achieve amazing things on a nightly basis. They constantly aspire to beauty and strive to be part of something they know is greater than themselves. Our musicians respond to violence with hope, they hold benefit concerts for food banks, they perform and serve in soup kitchens and their music is as relevant in the halls of cancer hospitals as it is in the world's greatest concert halls.

I have been on the road for ten years, and at times I have felt like Jack Kerouac. It has been an honor to be welcomed in your concert halls, your backstage lounges and your homes. I have heard performances I will never forget, like the Louisville Orchestra's *Nutcracker* just before they were locked out. They played like they might never play together again, and a piece that so many of us often play through in our sleep was performed with overwhelming emotion. Then this past May in San Juan, I heard one of the most joyful concerts I have ever attended, when the Puerto Rico Symphony played a program with music students from across the island in what is an annual event. It was humbling to be allowed to join them all backstage, and meet the parents of the students and witness the indelible role that the musicians of the orchestra play in the lives of so many.

I have traveled to visit with about 75% of our membership, and in being so welcomed in your concert halls I have constantly been aware that you have all been incredibly gracious to me, and I want you to know that I never once took it for granted.

There have been long nights, and the successes have been matched by bruises, but the musicians of our orchestras have pulled me through, and I have felt you all traveling with me everywhere I have gone. I have been amazed, inspired, and invigorated by your talent, your strength, your dedication, and your humanity.

In our troubled world, as we are assaulted with a 24-hour news cycle that too often sees human suffering as programming, humanity will always persevere in the face of violence, and music will forever be a response to hatred.

This we did with our lives for a reason. This is who we are. We are musicians, and we stand for beauty, peace, understanding, and compassion at a time when the world has never needed us more.

Also inscribed in stone at the nearby memorial for Martin Luther King are these words: "Make a career of humanity. Commit yourself to the noble struggle for equal rights. You will make a better person of yourself, a greater nation of your country, and a finer world to live in."

I want to thank you all for the friendship and support you have shown me in this decade, and I will miss you. After all of this time I still believe even more deeply in the message of hope that the musicians of our orchestras have articulated for the world. We have given our members things to work for, instead of only articulating things to work against. We have stood together as a united network of friends, we have been generous with each other, and we have been kind to those in need. I have no doubt that we will continue sharing the hope for the world that music provides. We will stand as a beacon of peace, inspiring our members and our audiences alike, and our music will remain an antidote for darkness. In this way musicians will always imagine, and will always work to realize, a more beautiful world.

Acknowledgments

Throughout my time as ICSOM Chair, and for many years before that, I have been fortunate to have the support of many friends throughout the world who have helped me to become a better writer, thinker and musician. As anyone who writes such a page of acknowledgments must feel, I worry that I might omit someone here, even as I acknowledge that there is no way I could possibly name everyone who has offered me new ideas to consider.

My largest debt of gratitude goes to every person who served as a member of the ICSOM Governing Board while I was Chair. The board received a first draft of everything we ever published, and every member of the board assisted in the editing process. The two musicians who served as Editor of *Senza Sordino* deserve special thanks, however. Richard Levine of the San Diego Symphony served as Editor from 2004 until 2014, and Peter de Boor of the Kennedy Center Opera House Orchestra assumed the role in 2014. I owe them both more than I can adequately express.

I'd also especially like to thank current ICSOM Chairperson Meredith Snow, along with the entire 2017-18 ICSOM Governing Board, for their gracious support of this book.

I was fortunate to work with some brilliant attorneys who served as ICSOM Counsel, and I've learned a great deal about the law, the orchestral field, and life from all of them. Leonard Leibowitz (who served from 1970 to 2010), Michael G. Okun (Interim Counsel 2009-2010), Susan Martin (2010-2015) and Kevin Case (2015-present). I am grateful to them all for their assistance in drafting these essays and speeches.

My two closest friends in the North Carolina Symphony, David Marschall and Elizabeth Lunsford, provided more support than can ever be repaid. Throughout the decade, through good times and bad times, they were constantly there for me with their support and advice, patiently listening to me and advising me as I worried over every issue that confronted ICSOM, and indulging me as I endlessly thought aloud about all that we were trying to achieve.

But as much as anyone, I am grateful to the orchestral musicians of North America and throughout the world, who graciously welcomed me into their concert halls and homes. I have been fortunate to have their support, and I am eternally grateful to them all.

And further, I'd like to thank every musician I have ever heard, in whatever field of music, whether we've ever met or not. My life has been enriched by every note.

Bruce Ridge

June, 2018

Courtesies

<ins>International Conference of Symphony and Opera Musicians (ICSOM)</ins>
All selections originally published in *Senza Sordino* appear here courtesy of the International Conference of Symphony and Opera Musicians.

The articles "The Autumn of Our Discontent: Orchestral Musicians and the Crisis in Arts Management" and "All the News That Fits the Print: The Failure of Arts Journalism at a Time of Cultural Need" were originally published at www.icsom.org and appear here courtesy of the International Conference of Symphony and Opera Musicians.

Note: the complete archive of *Senza Sordino*, the publication of the International Conference of Symphony and Opera Musicians (ICSOM), can be found on the ICSOM website at www.icsom.org/senza/.

<ins>American Federation of Musicians</ins>
- Supporting the Arts Empowers the Future (April, 2011)
- Music Brings Solace in the Face of Tragedy (February, 2013)
- A Teacher Remembered (June, 2014)
- Our Music Is a Statement for Peace (February, 2015)
- The Age of Incivility (February, 2016)
- Imagine a Better World (July, 2016)

Reprinted with the permission of the *International Musician*, the official journal of the American Federation of Musicians of the United States and Canada.

Boston Musicians' Association

Guest Editorial, Prelude: Boston Musicians' Association:
Originally published in the summer, 2011 edition of *Prelude*. Reprinted with the permission of the Boston Musicians' Association, Local 9-535 of the American Federation of Musicians.

League of American Orchestras

Perspective-Symphony Magazine
This article originally appeared in the winter 2012 issue of *Symphony*, the magazine of the League of American Orchestras, and is reprinted by permission.

Musicians of the Metropolitan Opera Orchestra

"2014: A Great Year for Orchestras (or haven't you heard?)" appears courtesy of the Musicians of the Metropolitan Opera Orchestra, originally published on www.metorchestramusicians.org

www.ingramcontent.com/pod-product-compliance
Lightning Source LLC
Chambersburg PA
CBHW031945170526
45157CB00002B/398